THE POWER OF DIGNITY

The Thoughtful Leader's Model for Attracting and

Keeping Stakeholders

Pete Geissler

"Treat people with respect and ...as the primary source of productivity gains."

Tom Peters and Robert Waterman, co-authors of *In Search of Excellence.*

"Leaders searching to unlock real excellence throughout their organizations will find imperative number one in this book." Bill O'Rourke, former President, ALCOA Russia, and now Executive Director, The Beard Institute, Palumbo-Donahue School of Business, Duquesne University.

"A must-read for managers who want to reap the many fiscal and psychic rewards of dignity in business." John Larsen, President Emeritus, New Balance Athletic Shoe, Inc. ; Director, NB (UK) Ltd.; and former president, World Federation of the Sporting Goods Industry (Lausanne).

Books from Pete Geissler
- The Power of Writing Well
- The Power of Ethics with Bill O'Rourke
- The Power of Dignity
- Divorce can be Such Sweet Sorrow
- Bigshots' Bull$^{*!@\#}$

Books from The Expressive Press
- VB.Net Web Development by Dr. Charles Wood
- The Little Black Book of Human Resources Management by Barry Wolfe

REVIEWS

RELEVANCE

"We've never forgotten that our committed associates and loyal customers were and remain instrumental to our becoming a global company. Managing for their dignity and satisfaction is the major driver of our success, and can be for others". John Larsen, President Emeritus, New Balance Athletic Shoe Company

"...a must-read book for all business starters, managers, supervisors, and owners...a wonderful, much-needed book." Gabriele Pillman, Associate Quality Engineer, Ergotron, Inc.

"...relevant...an excellent and timely message...I know from personal experience that employees are more valuable...than all the assets on the balance sheet...I am in total agreement." Victor E. Sower, PhD, CQE, Professor of Management, Sam Houston State University

MANAGEMENT STYLE

"This theme...represents a new and innovative approach to management style." Bob Deufel, President, Deufel & Associates

READABILITY

...forthright and refreshing...well-written...easy to read...a valuable self-improvement tool." L. David Weller, Professor Emeritus of Educational Leadership, University of Georgia

"...make no mistake; the words flow beautifully." Lynne B. Hare

Table of Contents

13. THE COMMON THREADS

Contributors to this book share many values, strategies, and tactics that contribute to success

14. EPILOGUE AND PROLOGUE: TOWARD UNIVERSAL ACCEPTANCE_

Spreading the word about Dignity can improve the public's and government's perception of business

About the author

PROLOGUE: THE PERFECT WIN-WIN, AND OUR SHARED PURPOSE

"THE DEEPEST HUNGER IN HUMANS IS THE DESIRE TO BE APPRECIATED." WILLIAM JAMES, 1842-1910, AMERICAN PSYCHOLOGIST AND PHILOSOPHER.

I've been on a wonderful and enlightening trip since I began researching this book in 2003 and published its first edition n 2004 as *Managing with Conscience for Competitive Advantage*. It was praised by reviewers for its importance, need, relevance, and style--see the back cover and Appendix II for details—prompting me to revisit and refine its premise.

During my research and writing I was fortunate to discover managers in a variety of businesses who actually understand and practice the awesome power of dignifying and respecting the people who depend on the businesses for their livelihoods, and on whom the businesses depend on for their existence—the perfect win-win. In addition, the profiled managers are totally convinced that dignity is the root cause of their firms' profitability and sustainability. I think you'll enjoy meeting them and profit from their insights.

This Book Is About New Possibilities for Individuals and Firms

This book examines, first, the very significant differences between managing for dignity and for stockholder value, then a number of successful businesses that are managed profitably and sustainably to protect and enhance the dignity of employees, customers, and other stakeholders, albeit in different ways and styles. The managers of those firms invariably ignore short-term accounting figures; they know that their businesses are much more than numbers and behave accordingly.

The evidence in favor of managing for dignity is largely anecdotal and empirical—which some philosophers opine is the source of all knowledge. I've added a smattering of statistical evidence by comparing such broad metrics as employees and customer retention in 2003 and 2013 for the businesses profiled PART II.

So you who are looking for the detailed quantifiable data of operating statements and balance sheets to validate the premise won't find it. Nevertheless, the experiences of the several contributors support what we like to call "conventional wisdom", and which the lawyers call "truth on its face". Perhaps I can call on our nation's founders for further support: "We hold these truths to be self-evident..."

If perchance I am ever reincarnated and need a job, I want it to be with one of the managers profiled in this book or their disciples, and I want to live by his/her principles. You'll know why after you've read further.

But first, a few definitions to be sure that we understand each other:

Dignity, noun, the state of being worthy of honor and respect; worthiness; high regard or estimation; self respect; importance.

Demean, verb, to debase, disdain, disrespect: the opposite of dignity.

MSV, Managing for Stockholder Value, noun, a management philosophy that tends to destroy dignity and firms via perverse, self-serving and short-term decisions by managers.

MBA-think, noun, another term for MSV, perhaps coined to lend MSV a bit of undeserved dignity.

Profitable growth, noun, another euphemism for MSV.

Source assets, *noun, employees and customers.*

Sustainable, *adjective, enduring, continuing, persistent.*

Sustain, *verb, to endure, continue, persist.*

PART I: SETTING THE STAGE

The search, the discovery, the consequences of demeaning MBA-think, and our shared and higher purpose to manage for the dignity of all stakeholders in order to earn reasonable profitability, sustain competitive advantage, and enrich the lives of all stakeholders.

Surely, that's not too much to ask and achieve.

1. THE SIMPLY SMART SEARCH FOR DIGNITY

EMPLOYEES, CUSTOMERS, AND OTHER STAKEHOLDERS ARE FAR MORE THAN EVERY BUSINESS'S MOST IMPORTANT ASSETS; THEY ARE THE SOURCE OF ALL OTHER ASSETS. TREAT THEM WITH THE DIGNITY THEY DESERVE AND PROSPER FINANCIALLY AND SOCIALLY.

That is the premise for this book.

I discovered it—I know, much has been written about the importance of people within and around any business. But, as far as I can determine, nobody has explained their importance as the source of all other assets, although I think that the concept is universally true.

I had my "aha" moment in the early 2000s as I was writing all sorts of corporate gargle—my endearing euphemism for marketing communications and public relations-- that paid lip service to the premise. Then I realized that many firms, including some that I consulted with, demean their sources assets and it has hurt and destroyed many lives, including several friends'. Examples abound:

I doubt that anybody in business of any sort or size could have missed reading the inflammatory headlines and sordid tales of corporate malfeasance and demise that have sensationalized the business press since the mid-nineties. ENRON's shady and covert financial manipulations to hide big losses, raise the price of its stock, and enrich its top executives—followed by its bankruptcy— perhaps made the loudest splash and became the nation's most notorious financial scandal. In 2006, CEO Jeffrey Skilling was sentenced to 24 years in prison for his role; then, in June 2013, I was appalled to learn that his sentence was reduced by 10 years based on a ruling that a sentencing guideline was improperly applied. I wonder how the former stakeholders who lost their careers and were bilked out of their savings feel about that.

ENRON didn't act alone: its executives were aided and abetted by its accounting firm, Arthur Andersen, whose executives must have been complicit or oblivious. The company, once a giant of accounting and management consulting, has joined ENRON in the corporate cesspool.

TYCO followed suit, with its top guns justifying huge bonuses and expenditures for artwork charged to the company. The nepotism and outright fraud at Adelphia Communications led to the arrest of the patriarch and his two sons, each of whom skimmed millions from the company's coffers. And Westinghouse Electric, a company with a household name and a long, enviable string of technological firsts that added greatly to our comfortable way of life, was mismanaged to a fire sale of its many and varied businesses, but not before the managers in charge fled with huge bonuses and pensions.

At this point, I must ask in all seriousness what the Board of Directors was doing as this drama unfolded. Were the members picked by management solely to rubber-stamp all management decisions? Were they cronies? Relatives? (Cronyism and nepotism were rampant at the time at lower levels, and maybe it had risen to the top.) I'll never know.

The company's virtual demise severely harmed the City of Pittsburgh and dozens of other cities and towns in which it operated, and, worse, it harmed countless lives.[1]

■■■

We could point to many causes of these and other failures and many of them would be gross rationalizations. For example, a former executive of one fallen company I know well is convinced that the company went belly-up because of onerous government regulations. He has conveniently forgotten that other similar companies are still living happily within those same regulations, and he has conveniently forgotten the greed and arrogance at the top, perhaps because a number of his friends were part of it.

The root cause of many failures—and the corrosive, corrupting force that destroys dignity—is that familiar goblin: managing for stockholder value, or an incessant drive for profitable growth, which is a euphemism for the same misguided mission of management. I've always abhorred that mission for all

---

[1] A professor of business told me that since the mid 1990s fewer than 100 companies have been charged with improprieties of some sort, less than one tenth of one percent of the publicly traded companies in the United States. He points to that one statistic as proof that the overwhelming majority of managers are honest, a leap of logic in my mind. Certainly there could be other reasons behind the small number of indictments.

sorts of reasons, but mainly because it serves top managers more than any other group. I and a growing number of people in my circle interested in business and its image actually consider managing for stockholder value to be amoral and a cruel hoax. We have become convinced that too many self-serving, short-sighted and, as a consequence, destructive decisions are made in its name—a conviction that is tackled throughout this book and by Jack Markowitz, an esteemed business editor at *The Pittsburgh Tribune Review.* He wrote in his column of July 25, 2013, that: "CEO pay, perks and stock options have inflated so wildly that rank and file workers have to grind their teeth at the unshared sacrifice of keeping companies competitive."

An early reviewer of this book suggested that managing for stockholder value and dignity can be compatible goals or drivers of policy—that they can live together in peace and harmony, but it is rare. When pressed, he could think of only one example: Paul O'Neill of International Paper and ALCOA. His guiding principle was safety of employees at all levels, which to me translates nicely to caring for their well-being, a big part of Dignity. During Mr. O'Neill's tenure at ALCOA, the accident rate throughout the company plummeted and the stock price soared ... which I think proves beyond any doubt that the premise of this book is valid. In fact, all the managers profiled in this book know that Dignity is the route to respectable profitability. Can MSV and Dignity live together harmoniously? You bet it can—if the driver is Dignity, not vice versa.

Early in 2004 The Harvard Business School agreed tacitly that managing for stockholder value is amoral: it started a semester-long course in ethics for its MBA students. In announcing the course, the dean said, reportedly with a shocked expression as if this revelation was brand new: "An unsettling number of business leaders apparently have put their own motives and profit before integrity." The University of Maryland has taken a different approach to the same subject; the business students tour prisons and interview white-collar criminals in an effort to scare them— the students, not the inmates—into some sense of integrity.

Perhaps not so strangely, the chairman of a giant manufacturer of electronic equipment said, after his predecessor's attempts at managing for stockholder value had failed and the stock price of his company dropped more than eighty percent, that "stock price is a byproduct (of good management); stock price isn't a driver. And any time I've seen any of us (presumably top managers) lose sight of that, it has always been a painful experience." I wonder if he feels the pain of the thousands of smaller investors who lost their shirts before he came to this revelation.

Strange, isn't it that the stakeholders that must be classified as big losers to the mission of stockholder value are the millions of smaller stockholders who were supposed to benefit. Other big losers are the towns and cities in which these companies operated, and all the local support businesses and their employees...customers who were forced to find other suppliers...employees who were forced to find other jobs and careers.

A former top executive at Westinghouse (one of the very good managers who was fired/retired because he tried to infuse some integrity into the company) asked me rhetorically how many millions of lives were disrupted or ruined because of the company's—management's—failure...how many divorces, lost college educations, postponed or cancelled retirements, resulted. I replied that I could think of at least a dozen such upsets in my small group of clients and friends. He could think of hundreds. Millions of personal trials and disasters is not hype by any means, and this from one of the smaller and less-publicized incidents, and perhaps one that showed the way for others.

He then asked me to write an entire book about these personal tragedies; "Management needs to know the results of its actions on the human condition," he mused. "You mean they don't know?" I asked with great disbelief. "I think that most managers, especially in larger companies, are so insulated from workers and communities that they don't have the foggiest idea of basic human suffering," he replied. Ouch.

A middle manager from PPG Industries who was downsized—in this case a euphemism for "replaced by a younger person who will work for a lower salary"—also suggested that I write an entire book on broken lives. "There are millions of us out there," he said, "and man*agers need to know the consequences of their actions, and how we feel about them."*

So I researched and wrote the following chapter to enlighten the unenlightened.

2. IF MANAGERS ONLY KNEW OR CARED. BROKEN COMPANIES, BROKEN LIVES

THE INCESSANT AND INSANE DRIVE FOR HIGHER PROFITS AND STOCK PRICES HAS SACRIFICED COUNTLESS LIVES.

The ENRON, WorldCom, Global Crossing, Kmart, Polaroid, Arthur Andersen, Qwest, Westinghouse and other debacles proved that regular employees, those who carry out the strategies of the higher-ups, lose the most when a company fails. They lose their jobs, pensions, savings plans and those stock options that executives promised would be their wealth of the future. Senior executives, directors, the big shareholders who are positioned to see the debacle coming—they typically escape with their wealth intact, and with lucrative pensions or jobs handed to them by the old-boy network.

The angst of lower-level employees is palpable. Most, if not all, felt that they had jobs for life, as they were told at their entrance interviews, and they lived accordingly, i.e., they saved little for the future simply because rock-solid companies and pensions/savings plans promised that the future would be both secure and comfortable.

While the notion of a job for life is considered terribly naïve these days when employees change careers or jobs at least six times during their working lives, it wasn't back in the fifties, sixties, and seventies when these people were hired; in fact it was a powerful incentive to come on board. Westinghouse, for example, had existed for about a century, and the company's primary business—the generation, transmission, distribution, and use of electricity—is so fundamental to our society that it was hardly imaginable that the company would not continue *ad infinitum*. In addition, Westinghouse had survived several serious close calls[2], disastrous management failures that put the company on the brink of

---

[2] Westinghouse's finances were severely strained during the fifties and sixties by a series of anti-trust violations, and during the seventies by long-term contracts to supply uranium fuel to utilities at unfavorable prices. Both crises were, clearly, egregious failures of management caused by an incessant drive for growth and profits.

bankruptcy, and that fact alone proved, by some stretch of logic, the company's resiliency and staying power. In fact, it proved that managers are not immune to greed and arrogance, and that the company could withstand only so many lapses in judgment.

A confession. I fell into the "resiliency trap" and paid for it dearly, if not disastrously. During the early nineties I was in a meeting of Westinghouse's financial gurus and the subject of the credit arms' bad loans came up. The opinion of one highly regarded attendee was that the losses are "far more serious than top managers are admitting in public," which of course is the way the top guns protected their jobs and stock options, at least temporarily. I had lived through a similar crisis—similar in that bankruptcy was bandied about—in the seventies, and could not believe that this so-called crisis would not be resolved and become just another bump in our fat, dumb, and happy road.

A few days after the meeting I reconsidered and talked to a respected competitor. "I'm diversifying," she said, "Westinghouse could very well be history, and soon." I believe in serendipity, and that conversation was enough to get me moving, albeit slowly, toward diversification of my client base. I opened negotiations for additional business with two other companies for which I was working sporadically and, during the following two years, contracts from them grew from about ten to forty percent of my revenues. When Westinghouse toppled, my revenue dropped by more than half, pretty traumatic but manageable for my small business, and far more palatable than a plunge to zero.

The City of Pittsburgh and surrounding towns (and literally dozens of similar towns throughout the United States in which Westinghouse had built plants) suffered greatly with Westinghouse's decline. At its peak, Westinghouse employed almost 20,000 in the Pittsburgh metropolitan area, 2,000 at its headquarters in downtown Pittsburgh. A rule of thumb is that every job in manufacturing creates three support jobs: doctors, lawyers, restaurant and government workers, writers like me, and so on. So some 60,000 people in Western Pennsylvania depended, at least in part, on Westinghouse for their livelihoods, a huge part of the population.

Many of these people took jobs in other areas; others coped with declining job opportunities and took "any old job" to stay in their hometown. The population of the city itself shrunk by almost half because of Westinghouse and other reasons, as did its tax base. As I write this, the city is "distressed," an official classification that is equivalent to being on the cusp of bankruptcy. Its bonds are rated junk, its political leaders are under attack for mismanagement, its lame-duck Mayor has virtually disappeared from public view as the FBI investigates the former Chief of Police, and its downtown is struggling to recover its vitality after retailers and other businesses either closed or moved to the suburbs. Yet, amazingly, the city and metropolitan area are consistently voted among America's Most Livable, and, in early 2013, America's Most Intelligent. I wonder why, and I wonder who's voting.

A frequent topic of conversation among those who are still here starts with, "Just think of how much better off the city would be if Westinghouse had survived." Or "if only Westinghouse had survived, just think of how our lives would be better." We express similar thoughts about the steel industry, but seem more willing to justify its shrinking as one effect of globalization, not mismanagement.

A former Westinghouse CEO rationalized that Westinghouse contributed greatly to the city. Yes, of course it did during the century or so that it was a viable company. It also contributed to society as a whole on a global scale, and we should, and do, applaud that. However, Westinghouse also contributed greatly to the decline of a once-proud city, and no amount of self-delusion or appreciation for the past can erase that simple fact.

The angst of employees as they dropped, singly and in groups, from the corporate tree was bolstered by a powerful disillusionment. They believed that managers actually work for the continuance of the company, not—I am not being too harsh here— to line their pockets. "Greed at the top" became a major topic of discussion in meetings, and, mostly, in less formal gatherings at bars and restaurants. Tempers flared, voices were raised, lawsuits were threatened, and too many drinks were downed.

While I can decry and condemn management's failures at Westinghouse, I cannot forget the company's many and significant philanthropic contributions. The company's support of The Pittsburgh Symphony, Opera, and the University of Pittsburgh come immediately to mind, and all improved the quality of life for many residents and added greatly to the city's reputation as a fine place to live.

Nevertheless, the damage of the company's demise, like a rampaging cancer, spread to homes. Spouses saw their lifestyles and dreams for the future shattered; some took to the bottle, others to the divorce courts. Children were told to forget Harvard, think community college or trade school or work after graduating from high school. The health of many deteriorated, as expected when stress soars and depression takes over. Some died—

including two of my closest friends-- from the stress and the booze they drank in a failed attempt to relieve it.

How many jobs and careers were lost, lives disrupted, families hurt, homes sold or repossessed, and educations sidetracked or foregone, stockholders broken? How many Great American Dreams had turned to Great American Nightmares? Several million is not an exaggeration. Following are several from my small circle. I've changed their names to protect their privacy.

**

Frank graduated in 1967 from what is now Carnegie Mellon University—when CMU was still Carnegie Tech—and the next day joined Westinghouse in the company's well-regarded management training program. His college studies focused on fine arts, and he was quick to draw people, buildings, bridges, whatever, and the drawings showed a flair for reality with a touch of the mystery that comes with an appreciation of Mary Cassatt and the other great impressionists.

The HR person told Frank at his entrance interview that he, Frank, would have a job for as long as he wanted it in the company's marketing communications group, where his talents could be used most effectively. All he had to do was display reasonable diligence and skill, which everybody knew was no great shakes for a graduate from a prestigious university like Carnegie Tech, and to behave with the highest integrity and morals; Westinghouse employees were a fun-loving group, but the line was drawn at a few drinks and golf games.

Eighteen months of training at six different divisions at six different locations landed Frank back in headquarters. The sign on his desk and the words on his business card said 'Communications Manager', and he set out to be one.

Life was good for the next twenty-five years: raises were bestowed on him steadily, reviews by bosses were consistently stellar, respect from peers and suppliers was unwavering. Nobody could blame Frank for feeling pretty comfortable with the straw in life that he had drawn. He supported his wives (yes, he stumbled his way through three) and his one daughter, and he indulged his loves of mid-sized cars, upscale golf, and top-shelf Scotch for his Rob Roys. To his discredit, he lived on the edge of financial meltdown, but so what? He believed it when the HR person said he had a job for life, his pension was secure, and he was riding high as a respected, even favored, employee.

Little did he know—how could he?—that he was living a dream within a house of cards called "managing for stockholder value".

Yes, Westinghouse went from paternalistic—an awful term for actually caring about the welfare and dignity of employees and customers—to caring more for the bottom line. The result was a series of bad management decisions related to a subsidiary's risky investments in real estate, followed by frantic spin-offs of healthy businesses to cover the losses, and then bankruptcy and a merger of the few remaining assets with CBS.

Frank lost his job when the division he was working for was sold to another company in management's mad dash to cook the books. He became redundant at age 48. He tried freelancing as a communications manager for a few years before realizing that he is a corporate animal in need of the structure and discipline of a larger organization.

He invested the little money he had saved in a concentrated job search aided by a top consultant. After six months of frantic but focused effort accompanied by extreme angst, he landed a job with a Westinghouse spin-off as the communications manager in the team marketing a new brand of products. "The best job I've ever had," he said often, "because my bosses let me be creative."

Sales and profits for his product line soared, and Frank's reviews were outstanding. He was named Marketer of the Year—only a few years before he was terminated again, this time at age 62.

The decision to terminate him was one of those perversities that can only be attributed to management's devotion to the bottom line.

Frank's product line, about fifteen percent of the company's revenues and an even higher percentage of its profits, was booming, but the remainder of the business was struggling. So top management cut headcount across the board rather than selectively, or, preferably, not at all if management could muster any faith in the future. The cuts came only a few months after the General Manager declared that employees are "our most important assets".

As I write this, Frank is struggling to maintain his sense of worth and his naturally jovial nature as he searches, for the second time in fifteen years, for a job that utilizes his considerable experience and talent. In the interim, he is toiling as a telephone interviewer for a marketing research firm for just over twice minimum wage, about one-third of his previous earnings and less than his needs.

**

During his twenty years with Westinghouse, Sam rose to creative director of the advertising group, in charge of investing a multi-million dollar budget to enhance the sales, profits, and image of the company.

When the company fell on hard times, the advertising budget was one of the first to be cut, in increments at first, then to zero. Sam became redundant and unemployed. "Best thing that could have happened to me," he said in a macho display of frustration and disdain for management. "Now I can get a job with a company that actually appreciates the strategic value of communicating with its many publics, and my talents to do so."

It turned out that being downsized wasn't the best thing for Sam after all. As he looked for that dream job, then any job at all in his field, he realized that his age, 50, was a liability despite laws that say it can't be. "Too many companies are convinced that the young bucks own the great ideas," he'd say. His position high on the corporate ladder, and his respectable salary, were also preventing him from getting a good job; he heard "overqualified" in many rejections, despite his willingness to start at a lower position and pay. He also complained that he was "tarred by the Westinghouse brush of failure," despite not having any direct part in it. "Who wants an ex-Westinghouse employee?" he'd ask.

He started to drink more heavily than ever, and his marriage, already shaky, finally fell apart. The bank foreclosed on his house, and he and his wife moved to separate, small apartments. His two children were denied the educations they had counted on and Sam had promised; Sam had graduated from a prestigious and very expensive liberal arts college and expected his children to follow in his footsteps. His daughter settled for a few selected courses at the local branch of a community college, and his son went to work as a server in a chain restaurant after graduating from high school. Disillusioned and disgruntled by the destruction of his dreams for the future, he, like his father, fell into the bottle.

Sam's life deteriorated in lockstep with the duration of his unemployment. His anger at the corporate world and its insensitivities to the plights of its employees became manifested in such declarations as: "employees are commodities like peas, to be chewed and spit out," and "employees are disposable, cattle to be exploited for the benefit of management," and "top managers who behave like those at Westinghouse should be in jail. They lived off us when we worked for them, and now we're broke and they're enjoying huge pensions and bonuses as some kind of fake reward for destroying a household name."

After several years of living by himself and a fruitless search for employment, Sam bought, for future royalties, the recipe for a pet food, and then arranged for interim financing. The business failed, and he moved to a smaller apartment, trading rent for minor repairs to other apartments owned by the same landlord, and he talked regularly of suicide. When his friends suggested counseling, he rejected it as being fraudulent.

Sam dove even deeper into the bottle and he died, alone, in his apartment.

At least four people are living lives that are far less fulfilling than what they envisioned, and management's failures were the triggering events.

**

"I'm a two-time victim of stockholder value," said Jim, a former vice president of marketing for a smaller manufacturer of electrical equipment used in commercial buildings and homes. Now in his late fifties, Jim had been searching for a job for almost a year after being let go the second time, and he was feeling the financial and emotional pain, as was his wife and two daughters, both of whom were attending a prestigious and expensive university.

"My first encounter was probably the less dramatic or traumatic. I directed the integration of a smaller company into a much larger one, which involved, among other things, combining two sales forces and replacing one nameplate with another. Please understand: the sole purpose of doing this was to cut costs by cutting employees at the expense of customer satisfaction. Convincing salespeople and customers that this was OK wasn't easy, especially when I was convinced that it was a bad business decision.

"Regardless, when the integration was complete, I was dispensable and was let go, as were hundreds of others."

Pete responds: "I wrote a speech for your president about that time. He wanted to convey his strategic vision to employees, and had scheduled a series of meetings around the country. I realized at our first meeting that what he really wanted to do was present a glowing financial plan. When I pointed out that he ignored such important considerations as opportunities for employees to grow into new management positions, and opportunities for customers to expand their business with the firm, he gave me that blank thousand-mile stare. I honestly think he didn't listen to or understand a word I said, and he presented his financial projections to very bored audiences. I know; I attended some of the meetings and watched as the attendees fidgeted."

Jim continued: "Yes, the president was following the corporate line that profits are everything, and the way to profits is to cut costs, mainly people costs. But, Pete, in a perfect example of executive arrogance, he'd take the corporate jet when a commercial flight would have been just as quick and convenient. He didn't cut the costs of his privileged position, and many employees saw the hypocrisy of that. I know I did.

"Anyway, I was unemployed for about six months before I landed at a huge company that had acquired a number of Westinghouse businesses, and merged them into their own. I started out as a product marketing manager, and then was promoted to a new position in strategic business development. When I took that job, I was told it was permanent.

"The company, which was honored only a few years earlier as one of the best-managed in the world, pigged out on risk. Debt rose to unconscionable levels, and the stock rose in lockstep. The parallels with Enron and Westinghouse are too close to miss.

"It was déjà vu all over again. As costs rose, mainly for servicing debt, cutting costs became the objective of management, and here I am, a year later, still looking for a job. Many of the top guys at the company, by the way, are either still at the top or living off their generous pensions. And smaller stockholders are licking the wounds of a fifty percent drop in the value of their holdings.

"My wife is now working to cover at least some of our expenses, and we are paying for others, including the educations of our daughters, with savings that we thought would be our retirement. We're thinking of selling our house, and we've become very careful about our so-called discretionary spending. The bottom line is that we've changed the way we live, and we can see more changes in the future.

**

Jack is a vice president of a nationwide consulting firm that specializes in outplacement of managers and professionals.

"Our business has changed dramatically over the past few years, and much of the change is the result of businesses cutting costs to raise profits, and their general disdain for employees. Severance packages have shrunk. For example, released employees, only a year or so ago, were given an average of six months of our services;

34

now they're given three to four months. The irony is that more time is needed these days to negotiate a new job. I find cutbacks like that to be just another example of the insensitivity to the human condition that is endemic with too many managers. Another example that I find even harder to live with is the sad reality that only fifteen percent of our corporate clients bother to contact us to ask how their former employees are doing. They've forgotten the very people who they once labeled their "most valuable assets", which is, of course, just another example of hypocrisy at the top.

"Dozens of people walk in here in various degrees of shock, disillusionment, and anger; almost all have been downsized or rightsized by companies looking to cut expenses to raise profits and stock prices. They've been hit by that relentlessly insane drive for a continuous string of higher profits.

"The extent of their psychological damage varies all over the lot. A few are quietly resigned to the situation; sometimes their angst bursts through their calm exteriors as the tensions of getting a new job increase. Most, however, are boiling mad with their self-esteem badly shaken. A big part of my job is to work with them to get back to their normal emotional state, which can take months, even years.

"A former corporate counsel was probably the angriest client I have ever handled. He was mature, in his late fifties, vigorous, in great health, at the top of his game. He had worked for the same company for almost thirty years, his entire working life, and he rose to be the top attorney. He lived the good life with his wife, two kids, a home in a leafy suburb, and a secure future.

"Then the CEO of his company decided to cut costs everywhere, to become "lean and mean", and heads rolled and damn the human consequences. The law department was reorganized and most of the work farmed out to a local firm. As a result, my client's position was eliminated.

"My client left with a year's pay and a bellyful of bad feelings. He needed another job with a corporation—he didn't have the experience or temperament for a job with an outside firm. Well, his timing was unfortunate: corporations were shrinking or dying in the area, but the law firms were expanding and doing just fine. He and his family were enmeshed in the social fabric of their neighborhood and the city, and, initially, moving to another city was not an option. However, after about six months of fruitless searching, he decided to consider other locations—over his wife's very vociferous objections.

"Desperate by this time, he accepted a job in a much smaller city, and it turned out to be a big mistake. After only a month or so on the job, he realized that he didn't fit the culture of the company or the city, and he became increasingly uncomfortable. He lost much of his self-esteem again, sure that he could not even be trusted to decide on something as simple as the right job, and his wife, back in his home city, wasn't much help in restoring his emotional center. She tried, but her unhappiness at the prospect of moving showed despite her best efforts to hide it.

"The bottom line is that this man died of a heart attack in his motel room in the city that he had hoped would be his new home. His wife is totally convinced that the stress of a job that didn't fit his nature, added to stress of looking for employment, killed him. She could very well be right.

**

Jack tells his own story: "In hindsight, I was one of the more fortunate victims of managing for stockholder value. I landed on my feet after two episodes, one divorce, the alienation of my daughter, and the cusp of bankruptcy. Sounds like more of a daytime soap than a life, but that's what happened.

"I was the vice president, human resources, for a large regional financial organization, living a pretty idyllic life in a small city, when one of the behemoths of the industry made the handful of owners an offer they couldn't refuse, a.k.a. big bucks. The acquirer offered me a senior HR job in its headquarters, a job with far broader responsibilities than I had, and, not seeing a good alternative, I accepted.

"It was mistake #1. I guess you could say that the move was a step up in responsibilities and pay, but a huge drop down in compatibility. My new employer was addicted to the bottom line, and I never could accept that management style; no wonder I became unhappy, edgy, and angry.

"So, a few years later I quit and accepted another HR job, this time with an old-line, closely held manufacturer with the highest reputation for quality of its products and esteem for its employees and customers. It turned out to be mistake #2.

"The company was sold a few months later, for big bucks again, to what I graciously call a band of corporate thieves and rapists. I knew I wouldn't fit when the new president said to me: "The only way to track employees is to put deer tags in their ears." I couldn't believe his lack of compassion and respect.

"As you'd expect, the company was pillaged—its better businesses sold to line the pockets o the new owners—and was soon half the size it was when I joined it. Hundreds of employees, some with thirty years of valuable, hard-to-find experience and knowledge in a very specialized business, were let go; the company decimated its most important assets, its seed corn, and its future. The value of people wasn't considered. It was a cesspool of alligators, this disdain for people and for the continuity of the business. Customers fled the sinking ship.

"I was among those cut. 'You've done a great job; you're just not part of our team', I was told was the reason. What a farce! I can't to this day accept or understand that kind of rationalizing—it reminds me too much of government when one party takes over from the other and people are let go because of their party affiliation, not their abilities or contributions.

"Here I was, in my forties and angrier, more fearful, more anxious, than ever, depressed and convinced that I could not make even the simplest decisions and be sure that they were right. I was angry at myself, my former employers who had betrayed me, and all of corporate America for its ethical lapses.

"I took my anger out on my family and friends simply because they were handy. Biggest mistake #3: my wife and I divorced, my daughter avoided me at the very vulnerable age of ten, and my finances tanked. Angrier than ever, I made my next bad decision and started a consulting business with my few remaining funds and a partner. Mistake #4. We did OK for a few years, before my partner dropped out and our biggest client left because of a long strike. I tried and failed to breathe life into the business with too little cash and a couple of remaining employees. I almost lost my house, and my financials were a disaster.

"Now, late in my career, I love my new job and my new wife, and, after some fifteen years of alienation, my daughter and I are getting along just fine. With all that, I suppose that I am one of the luckier victims of management greed, but..."

**

Mary, a chief psychiatric nurse at a large mental health hospital, has "seen it all", meaning that she has seen the devastating mental and physical damage heaped on workers who have lost their jobs, and on their families who feel the reverberations. The damage seems especially severe if the reasons for unemployment were management's malfeasance. "They seem better able to understand their plights if they lost their jobs because of a downturn in the economy, for example, maybe because such causes are acts of God

40

and they've lived through a few. They are confused, betrayed, and enraged when they feel that bad management was the cause."

Mary specializes in rehabilitating people with emotional illnesses brought on by severe trauma. "I've seen literally hundreds of patients who have been traumatized by being downsized, to use the cliché of the day. Most of my patients are men; women seem better able to cope with the loss of a job. And many of them are skilled, blue-collar, unionized workers who expect the company to value their expertise, and the union to protect their rights and wages.

"The trauma typically brings on or exacerbates four problems: drinking, divorce, disease—both mental and physical—and debt. The four 'Deadly D's'.

"I live in a small town outside of Pittsburgh in which Westinghouse was by far the major employer. The Westinghouse plant employed several thousands, many the second and third generations of families that depended on the company for their livelihoods. They were fiercely loyal to the company, and figured that the company was equally loyal to them.

"Not so. As everyone knows by now, Westinghouse disappeared for what they perceive to be the wrong reasons, and workers' loyalty and security turned to bitterness and hate, anger and despair.

"A case in point: A close friend of mine was married to a second-generation plant worker who lost his job in the late eighties, when he was only forty-five years old. This man, who had spent years developing and honing his well-paid skills, lived for his job and the respect it gave him. When he lost his job, he lost his self-respect and his ego support. Always a loner, he became more introverted than ever, and, finally, in despair, took a job washing windows at pay and skill levels far below what he was used to. He became depressed and started to drink heavily to relieve the symptoms, making him even more depressed in that never-ending circle of self delusion and destruction. He became edgy, then downright nasty as he became more drunk. He and his wife fought over trivial matters, and he was often physically abusive.

"The wife took a job for the first time in her life, opening a whole new and friendlier world for her. She urged her husband to get psychiatric help, but he was too proud for that. She finally left him and found a new place to live.

"I suppose the good news is that he survived two serious heart attacks, and, at sixty, is working at another menial job. His wife is struggling to make ends meet. Two of their four children dropped out of a public college, and one is a confirmed alcoholic at age 26.

Not a pretty picture, but maybe prettier than the plight of a family that I'll call the Smiths.

"Mister Smith lost his job at a glass plant nearby, and, as he became more and more angry about it. He also became more and more of an abusive drunk. He drank at home, at his social club, at friends' homes—anywhere he could get his hands on booze. Drinking led to petty arguments with his wife, which escalated and broadened to slugfests with his wife and family. One day he almost choked his teenage daughter to death. The wife feared for her and her daughter's lives, and her daughter escaped to a friend's house.

"It's so easy to get drunk in this town, where it seems that every other doorway on Main Street is a dirt bar that has become a social club for the disenfranchised. When they were employed, the men would stop at one bar or another for a relaxing beer on the way home. Now that they don't have anything to do, they just stop anytime of the day at a favorite bar to drink and grouse about their lot in life, and to fritter away the few dollars left from their savings and small pensions. It's all so destructive.

"Visibly drunk a good part of the day, Mister Smith couldn't hold even a menial assembly line job. Nobody—except maybe Mister Smith himself-- was surprised when he came down with severe problems with his pancreas, which some folks around here called poetic justice. His doctor told him to quit drinking or be dead in six weeks. He stopped for a week or two, and then went back into the bottle as deeply as ever. I guess he didn't figure he had anything left to live for. Isn't that a form of slow suicide? We're waiting for him to die as I'm telling his story.

"Missus Smith found a job that paid the bills and little else, and then left to live in her own apartment. She now works two jobs, and is recovering from what is commonly called a 'nervous breakdown'. Her credit card debt has put her on the cusp of bankruptcy.

"Drinking, divorce, disease, and debt. All might have happened without unemployment; there's no way to know, but the unemployment was the trigger, wasn't it?

"The Power of Dignity...nice title for a book, one that applies as well to another patient of mine, a happier ending than the two patients I've already discussed. He was involuntarily retired—the big boys call it attrition in some misguided attempt at humanity—in his late forties from a U.S. Steel plant, and he was convinced that his life was over. Angry, depressed, and disillusioned, he took to the bottle, a familiar escape route by now. He'd stay up all night watching TV and drinking to the point of senseless oblivion.

"After a year or so of this destructive behavior his live-in girlfriend kicked him out of the house, and he tried to commit suicide, which got him automatically committed—it's the law—to the hospital where I work. After three weeks of group therapy—which, uncharacteristically, he accepted wholeheartedly—he realized he was in trouble and reversed his destructive behavior by cutting his drinking back to the occasional beer, and his self-pity to a quiet confidence.

"The good news is that he bounced back to his former self, his girl friend welcomed him back into their house, and he's working steadily."

**

I added two of my more egregious examples: A friend and client, age 59, was named Communications Manager of the Year and he basked in the bonus and glory; six months later he was fired and replaced by a younger employee who was paid considerably less, an obvious case of age discrimination with the sole purpose of cutting costs. My friend threatened to sue; the company lawyer said "go ahead; it will be years and thousands of dollars before your suit gets to court." How demeaning can you get? My friend had no choice but to reinvent his life; he lived on his meager pension for a year before landing a menial job that he hates and which pays about one-third of what he earned as a manager. He is trying desperately to hold on to his dignity.

Another friend fared a bit better. She ran the payment department at a huge utility and she did it so efficiently that she was cited by the company and by a national trade association for her management and people skills, A short time later the company merged with another and some misguided manager outsourced the function in his fervor to impress the Public Utility Commission by cutting headcount—surely one of the more obscene terms in business--and fifteen employees lost their jobs. My friend found another job with a small accounting firm at a reduced salary; several of her former employees weren't so fortunate and were unemployed for years.

I could go on, but I'm sure I've made my point and case. So let's move to the positives of dignity and my proposed new management direction that is based on it.

3. PROPOSED: A NEW DIRECTION, A NEW WAY TO THINK ABOUT ASSETS AND SUSTAINABLE COMPETITIVE ADVANTAGE

THE UNCANNY POWER OF YOUR SOURCE ASSETS

"We must build a new world, a far better world---one in which the eternal dignity of man is respected." Harry S. Truman, April 23, 1945.

The highest—perhaps most idealistic-- purpose of this book is to act on Truman's challenge to the World, which in my view remains unmet—the subject of another book.

A more fundamental and perhaps more attainable purpose, and an important step toward meeting Truman's challenge, is to suggest a management direction that could prevent more of the same failings described earlier.. The suggested direction could restore a sense of trust and humanity to management that, the headlines tell us, seems so lacking. The consensus of those managers who have contributed to this book is that many of their peers, particularly in smaller organizations, already are guided by the new direction, just as they are. They also lament that all managers do not follow suit simply because it seems so simple, successful, humane, and, yes, dignified.

To that end of a more universal acceptance, I suggest this new direction that is the best of all worlds: reasonable profits that raise stock prices, plus continuity of the business—the new buzzword is sustainability-- that benefits all stakeholders... The new direction recognizes clearly the basis, the rationale, the premise put forth in CHAPTER 1: **Employees, customers, and other stakeholders are far more than every business's most important assets; they are the source of all other assets. Treat them with the dignity they deserve and prosper financially and socially.**

■ ■

Perhaps that thought is self-evident to many readers, but surely not all and surely not at a conscious level. So I want to remind all of us that employees and customers aren't really assets in the sense that stockholders own them[3], or banks have used them for collateral against loans. But nobody can deny that they are assets nevertheless. In fact, many annual reports and speeches by executives affirm, in words that have become clichés, that employees and customers are the company's most important assets.

The two assets are irretrievably joined at the brain in the tightest of mutual dependencies. Sustainable Competitive Advantage is a product of employees who work with dignity to achieve it; all the managers who have contributed to this book know that intuitively.

I fleshed out the idea that employees and customers are the sources of all other assets and ran my eyes down the balance sheets in several annual reports.

---

[3] Robert S. Kaplan and David P. Norton wrote, in "Measuring the Strategic Readiness of Intangible Assets, (Harvard business review, February 2004) that: "Measuring the value if such tangible assets is the Holy Grail of accounting. Employees' skills, IT systems and organizational cultures are worth far more too many companies than their tangible assets... are hard for competitors to imitate, which makes them a powerful source of competitive advantage..."

Factories, buildings, machinery and equipment—all the tangible assets—all spring directly from customers who pay for products and services. No customers, no tangible assets. Simple.

Patents, copyrights, research, product knowledge—the intangible assets, the so-called intellectual property—are all in the heads of employees, not file cabinets or computer memories. Lose those employees, lose the business. My small business is the perfect example, as you'll see in Chapter 9. If what's in my head is lost, the business is lost as well.

I moved to the operating statement—revenues, profits, salaries, dividends—all directly from customers. I paused at "working capital". Perhaps I could argue that capital—especially initial capital—emanates from the financial markets, including banks and investors of whatever stripes. The counter argument would be that the markets are eager to fund a startup business that is based on a good idea—which of course is held in the head of one or a group of employees. Can you name a business that wasn't started with an idea, aka an intellectual epiphany or insight?

The markets are equally eager to finance a going concern with a positive cash flow, a result of customers who send checks. So perhaps it's not a stretch to say that capitalism itself is based on employees and customers! Was that what Peter Drucker had in mind when he reminded us that the first legitimate purpose of every business is to find and serve a customer? And could he have completed the thought by adding: and the employees needed to meet that purpose?

My conclusions: First, that the two major assets of any business are employees and customers, and all other assets are minor in that they fall out from the major. And second, that all businesses should be managed to maximize the dignity of employees and customers. Simple, but...

Many businesses I know appear to be managed to demean employees and customers. . Consider...

Customer service is now often the responsibility of the customer. Customers pump their own gas, wash their own windshields, and check their own oil, mocking the outmoded term "service station" and replacing it with "self-service station". We customers wade through tedious menus on the phone to get to other menus ad nauseum in an irritating effort to solve our own problems or buy a product or make an appointment, and so on.

Surprisingly, companies and individuals in service businesses seem to be leading the way in this draconian and demeaning practice. For example, calling my group of five doctors drops me into the never-never land of a long menu, wasting my time with irrelevance. My accountant's two-person business is even worse. The menu rarely relates to my needs, so I am forced to hang on the line to the long-winded end of its harangue, when a real person picks up; why didn't the menu offer the option to go there directly, or why didn't she pick up first? I know, follow the money and nuts to the caller.

The company from which I bought my computer is legendary for menus designed to be understood only by the techies of the world, a label that will never apply to me or to the millions like me, so we are second-class customers.

I could go on and on, and, alas, you no doubt can come up with dozens of examples that irritate more than satisfy. They all make it harder, more infuriating, and more demeaning to do business.

Employees of firms both large and small that I know gripe constantly about their jobs. My clients are good examples. The most favorable—and decidedly backhanded—comment I've heard for the past ten years at least was "if I must work, this is as good a place as any." Not much dignity or respect in that kind of resignation. My best client complains loudly and frequently that his company is wildly dysfunctional, his word for the mountains of paperwork, almost all of it related to costs, he needs to complete before he has time to think about and do his real job, the one by which his performance is measured. Where's the dignity in that?

By the way, he complains loudly that he doesn't have time to think, he is so immersed in paperwork. When he slips into that mode, I ask him, "What else are you being paid to do? Isn't thinking your only job?" He doesn't have time to think of an answer, or even to see the irony.

His high-tech company, with annual sales of almost $2.5 billion, adds to the irony with its Help Desk, an employee-only internal website. Designed to "make it easy"—that's what the brochure says—to find and understand the inner workings of pension plans, health insurance and the like, it actually adds to employees' frustration and anger by confronting them with a long and convoluted menu that prompts most to hang up, unfulfilled. Finding a human with helpful information is, in fact, not on the menu. Nobody is behind the desk.

At a local department store recently the sales lady struggled with the cash register and apologized, "We were given new cash registers but weren't trained to use them, so I'm sorry for the delay." "Why do you want to apologize for bad management?" I asked. "I can think that, not say it." Ouch, again.

A friend who is a VP for a huge engineering firm lives in a world of management contradictions. On the one hand, his superiors push him to bill more hours to create a larger revenue stream; on the other, these same managers push him to establish and keep long-term relationships with major customers. He is torn between tactical and strategic imperatives and is looking for another job with a company that understands and lives by its mission.

I've written many speeches for top managers who recite, explicitly or implicitly, that tired cliché "employees (or customers) are our most important assets." Then, usually a short time later, the anonymous company—never the manager by name—announces it will downsize or rightsize or no longer serve a market that doesn't fit with the company's strategy for growth of revenue or profits. Am I the only one to see the demeaning hypocrisy it unleashes on employees and customers alike? See my book *BigShots' BullShit* for more on this demeaning practice.

Not long ago I wrote a speech for the CEO of a major, Dow 30 manufacturer with sales in the area of $12 billion. The audience was some two thousand executives of a customer group that the company had served for a century, and who contributed at least thirty percent of the company's revenue and a slightly lesser percentage of profits. The essence of the message was that the manufacturer would no longer serve this group because prices and profits were too low and the CEO had better places to invest.

Everybody in the room knew what this short-sighted CEO really meant was, simply, that "there are better places to raise the value of my stock options". The audience squirmed and laughed, silently to be polite, and proceeded to purchase from the several competitors both here and abroad. That manufacturer is no longer in business, and the CEO, when I met him a few years later at a cocktail party, defended his moves as "good for the city, good for investors". I wonder how this man, obviously spaced out on Planet Denial, could find any good in destroying or disrupting the lives of, literally, millions of loyal employees, customers, investors, and suppliers, including me and dozens of my good friends.

Here's the powerful imperative that many managers accept reluctantly or not at all:

The way to increase revenues, profits, and shareholder value is to stop obsessing on them and obsess instead on their sources.

Not easy: Investors, directors, and brokerage firms monitor and reward managers who work on their behalf using such destructive short-sighted metrics as quarterly earnings, the very essence of MBA-think.

To expand, these same managers ignore leading indicators such as the firm's record of employee and customer turnover, the very metrics that create long-term value. So when you hear or read that the board of directors has justified the outsized compensation packages of top executives because there simply isn't enough good talent available, you can be virtually certain that the board is overseeing (a cruel joke in too many firms, I fear) a company focused on the short term.

In fact, there is no shortage of MBA-think executives; the b-schools graduate thousands every year. There is a shortage of talented executives who can create lasting value and, at the same time, satisfy the board's and Wall Street's unrealistic and, ultimately, destructive objectives.

Based on the profiles in this book and on several other studies--refer to APPENDIX I: SUGGSTED FURTHER READING--firms that are managed in ways that treat employees and customers with dignity:

- outperform their peers on the stock market or, if privately held, are reasonably profitable and share their profits with employees and customers;

- encourage the positive relationships between managers and other employees with open, honest communications and benefits such as continuous learning;
- Eschew short-term profits in favor of long-term value.

Other writers have expressed similar thoughts: *But common sense suggests, and empirical studies show, those organizations that create deeper loyalty—with employees, customers, and investors— experience more sustained success. In this age of commoditization, one of the truly differentiating characteristics of leaders and companies is the quality and durability of the relationships they create."* Chip Conley, author of *PEAK* and funder and CEO of Joie de Vivre hospitality.

...companies face mounting pressures to prove themselves worthy of their employees, customers, and investors. In order to do so, they must combine competitive savvy with a genuine desire to do more that maximize short-term profits or enrich a narrow circle of stakeholders. Laurie Bassi

et al, authors of *Good Company*.

4. THE INVISIBLE CHASM THAT SEPARATES MANAGEMENT STYLES

MANAGING FOR STOCKHOLDER VALUE AND LEADING WITH DIGNITY SHARE VERY LITTLE COMMON GROUND

"American business needs a lifting purpose greater that the struggle of materialism." Herbert Hoover

I learned long ago that universal truths and clear-cut answers are rare, perhaps nonexistent. Therefore, Dignity as the point or overarching strategy may not be for every manager, every company. That said, I am quick to point out that <u>NO</u> management philosophy or style is an island unto itself; each is surely tempered by any number of ancillary or supporting considerations that are beyond the scope of this book. Balance—and how managers tip the balance—is the name of the game.

For example, I was told by a director that, years ago, the managers of Motorola once tipped the balance so steeply toward Dignity in the form of coddling customers that managers neglected to invest in upgrading a major product line. The company slid from first to third place in the market, sales and profits plummeted, and a new management team is fighting to keep the company in business.

I can say that tipping the balance toward dignity works very well for me and the

firms within and near my circle, as the profiles in the book demonstrate. The other side of that same coin is that MSV and MBA-think have been destructive to many of the companies that practice it (or did for those no longer with us), as discussed earlier. Damaged or destroyed as well are the reputations of businesspersons themselves who worked for those companies— including those who were not involved directly in some of the debacles but who become guilty by association. If high tides lift all boats, low tides drop all of those same boats. (I asked a former high-level executive of a disgraced company to write a review of this book so that I could quote him. He refused: "My obvious tie to this company would harm sales and credibility of the book, not help.")

Writing this book has confirmed to me that many positive and constructive results drop out of dignity, little positive or constructive out of stockholder value. Some specifics:

1. *Dignity* **encourages long-term, strategic thinking and behavior**—which is espoused and applauded by every manager I know—for several reasons. Perhaps the first—and most elusive—is that it's very difficult to think short-term when the very lives and lifestyles of people are considered, unless, of course, managers can't muster any empathy for their fellows. One interesting corollary is that empathic managers create meaningful, interesting jobs that involve employees in the welfare and future of the business. (ESOPs are good examples.) You'll find impressive examples of this throughout this book.

Another is that monthly or quarterly operating statements are either ignored completely or given a gratuitous glance.

The 'bottom line' for these managers is zero to little turnover of employees and customers, highest product quality, and the lower costs and higher profits that they are convinced will surely result.

MBA-think, on the other hand, encourages short-term thinking and behavior; it gives executives draconian incentives to inflate stock prices to raise their options' value, to avoid considering anything but pecuniary gain. Decisions are made that inflate, aka distort or lie about, revenues and profits; witness ENRON and Arthur Andersen, and, in my direct experience, Westinghouse and Dravo Corporation. Plant managers at Westinghouse—and, I'm told, at many other manufacturers—would routinely ship product at the end of a month and before it was ready because, in the misguided and misleading accounting system in place, the revenue and profit expected from that shipment could be booked as soon as the truck or railroad car left the shipping dock. Never mind that the customer would be unhappy with partial shipments or shoddy products; the service department could fix that later, at horrific expense, of course. Quality and customer satisfaction, which are of course birds in the same nest, went by the wayside, and surely so did long-term profitability.

A friend, a brilliant engineer who rose to one rung below the very top of Dravo, a huge engineering/construction company, fell into an analogous trap. Under extreme pressure to grow—pressure applied by an overly ambitious CEO brought in from outside the company by an equally ambitious board—my friend negotiated (actually, "bought") projects valued at hundreds of millions of dollars, knowing full well that the contract prices were so low that the company could not possibly book the profits projected. My friend figured he'd make it up with the extras, a risky but occasional strategy in construction

The euphoria of booking big contracts led, in a few years, to the desperation of saving the company, then to bankruptcy and the disappearance of yet another corporate icon

The New York Times of February 7, 2004, in an article titled "Survey Finds Profit Pressure Leading to Poor Decisions", cited a Study by Duke University and the University of Washington that concluded that "short-term often eclipses the long-term—more than half the companies surveyed said they would delay starting a project to meet their earnings target, even if they knew it to be profitable. About eighty percent said they would cut spending on research and development, advertising, or maintenance that would not hurt them in the short run but could hurt them over time—to meet quarterly earnings goals." Then, in some sort of perverse attempt to bestow some integrity onto management, the article stated, "Only about ten percent of the companies surveyed said they would alter their accounting assumptions to meet a quarterly target, and only about twenty percent said they would postpone making an accounting change to meet a target." (The emphases are mine, because I would have written "an amazingly and disturbingly high percentage of the companies surveyed...

I was lunching with a director of marketing at Westinghouse and said, "Long term planning at Westinghouse is deciding what to have during the next coffee break." "You have too long a view," he replied. "We work hard on strategic plans and then put the documents on a shelf to collect dust, and then it's back to business as usual, minute by minute, fire by fire."

2. *Dignity* **managers are concerned about costs, as any manager should be**. But, because of their longer-term thinking, they plan for the time when costs can be converted to revenue and profit. An example: Jim Browne at Allegheny Financial doesn't expect certain new hires to contribute to revenue and profits for three to four years, then expects stellar performance, and gets it, for many years afterward. And Ron Herring at Mine Safety Appliance Company says that it takes eighteen months for an employee to "get traction; and two years to really understand his or her job. We gladly take the short-term hit in anticipation of the long-term gain." I place both managers as the epitome of sustainability.

MBA-think, on the other hand, encourages cutting costs to raise profits and stock prices for the short term. In the long run, operating in that way actually costs big time, not only in money but also in bankruptcy. Ken Lovorn, in Chapter 11, tells of the president of a billion dollar engineering company who managed by cutting heads when business was slow, then adding them when business improved. The costs to terminate and rehire were astronomical, especially in this cyclical business, and product quality suffered greatly as well. Which brings up a good point: strategic thinking requires faith that the future will be better or as good as the past, and cycles will level out.

3. ***Dignity* encourages win-win, team work, a culture of cooperation and equality.** Jim Browne's team (one member calls it "family" with perfect justification) is a stellar example: all members share the profits and security of a successful business, and customers win with extraordinary service that extends well beyond money management. Decisions are made by the team, yet each member enjoys a strong autonomy. Frank, the enterprising bartender with a phenomenal memory who is discussed in Chapter 6, created, almost single-handedly, a win-win culture in an entire hotel. And Kerotest, in Chapter 10, stipulates in its union contract, that, "if you can't work in a team, you can't work at Kerotest."

MBA-think, on the other hand tends to create win-lose, a culture of adversity, extreme personal competitiveness and

divisiveness. *Employees tend to do what is asked by bosses, rather than what is right for the business; the shipping policies at many companies are a good example. And a culture of divisiveness is common, although at times I wonder if employees know it in their eagerness to embrace management's decrees.*

I was lunching with a director of distribution at PPG Industries when he began to extol the virtues of managing for stockholder value. I asked him if he thought it was fair for his boss and his boss's boss and so on up the chain to be rewarded with options for hundreds and thousands of shares of stock when his options were limited to fifty or a hundred shares. He stopped to think about that, I swear for the first time, before he answered that yes, it was fair, because those guys made more money than he did. I asked, very softly, if they worked harder, longer, smarter. No answer. I wondered why this intelligent man had bought into a system of compensation that was, to me, so lopsided.

4. ***Dignity* encourages creativity, entrepreneurism.** The culture of dignity encourages a free exchange of opinions, values, and thinking—not only among employees, but also among employees and customers. The cornerstone of Jim Browne's and Ron Herring's management style is LISTEN—to customers first, because only then can employees understand customers' problems, needs and

wants, and then to other employees as minds mesh for creative solutions and services. And a cornerstone of Ken Lovorn's style is his customer advocate, whose primary job is to listen to customers—to look at every project and issue from the customer's point of view, then to be certain that employees doing the work understand it. I doubt if my friend with the construction company would have signed those losing contracts if he felt free to discuss what he was doing with the chairman, or if he had listened to what his estimators were saying.

The stifling of creativity by MBA-think is amply illustrated by the engineering company that prompted Ken Lovorn in Chapter 11 to start his own shop. The high-level employees listening to the president were so intimidated—Ken wasn't—that they actually approved, by their silence, a strategy that was obviously misdirected. Yet I'm sure that each knew a better way that at least could have saved the company.

5. ***Dignity inherently demands that customers receive more than they expect,*** thereby creating the strongest possible competitive advantage and the highest possible percentage of repeat business (and lowest costs for sales and marketing). One of my clients asserts that "customer satisfaction" is too mild a concept for

managers who understand its power; "delight" is more appropriate. Without exception, all of my clients have come to expect more than text from me; they also expect a hospitable environment that encourages creativity. All the contributors to this book have literally built their businesses around exceeding expectations.

MBA-think, on the other hand, inherently demands that the terms of contracts and agreements be met to the letter, or as *close to the letter as possible. Anything more adds to immediate costs, and that is culturally unacceptable.*

PART II: PROFILES OF PRACTITIONERS

Oliver Wendell Holmes said that the best test of an idea is its power to be accepted in the competitive market.

Such is the case with Dignity as the focus of management. The idea has been espoused and applied successfully by the following companies and managers for years, and the results ... well, read on and be impressed.

5. INVESTMENTS. NOT THE HALF OF IT FOR THIS FINANCIAL PLANNER

LISTEN. IT'S THE PROFITABLE SOUND OF SUCCESS VIA SATISFIED EMPLOYEES AND CUSTOMERS.

IN 2004, Jim Browne was the managing partner of Allegheny Financial Group, a financial services company that he helped found in the 1970s. He was, and remains, an interesting enigma. He devoted the first decades of his adult life to the priesthood, where he renounced all worldly goods and espoused religion. When he reached middle age, he left the priesthood to manage money for others and, along the way, to amass considerable money and other worldly goods for himself, his wife, and his children.

The group functions in three areas that are managed as separate entities to avoid conflicts of interest: financial planning[4], private equity, and investment brokerage. With just under 200 employees and associates, the group is the largest of its kind in Western Pennsylvania. Its financial planning group—the focus of this success story--has been designated by Worth Magazine as among the best money managers in the nation.

Jim describes his planning business: "The ads we've run for years in various performing arts magazines here in Pittsburgh always describe our business in these terse words: Allegheny Financial provides asset management services for successful individuals, businesses and pension plans. In fact, we do much more—we help customers enrich their present lives in all sorts of ways and plan their lives for the enriched future they envision. I purposely use the word 'enrich' because it implies money, of course, and much, much more. And I want to point out that the operative word is 'help'; we don't impose or dictate to people we think of as our partners. I'll flesh out these ideas later."

---

[4] In the parlance of this company, "planning" encompasses setting the direction and focus of investing, the actual placing of funds, tracking performance, and adjusting the asset mix as conditions change over time.

Our long-Term Value is in Our Employees' and Customers' Minds

"We're a typical service business in that the value of our physical assets is virtually insignificant to our balance sheet or operating statement. Those assets include our equity in a small building that we own, and in the furniture, computers and so on that we use every day.

"The value of our intangible assets is the inestimable value of our employees' and customers' minds. They are, in the truest sense, the company, and, of course, given today's accounting rules, they don't show up on any of our financial statements. Nevertheless, my partners and I know their value and behave accordingly.

"We agree that we operate our business with one umbrella principle: give customers more than they expect, and—the obvious corollary—hire employees who are able, intellectually and emotionally, to do that.

"Deciding how to give customers more than they expect is the easy part. Finding employees to do that is far more difficult and is our highest barrier, one that, despite our best efforts, we haven't yet learned to hurdle completely. Yes, we explain our philosophies during the initial interviews, and candidates nod and say that they understand and can work happily within them. Nevertheless, we see, far too often, some sense of discontentment replace the original sense of excitement during the first eight weeks of employment. That's followed by a sense that this relationship can't work, and either our new employee resigns or we ask him or her to go.

"So our employee turnover rate during the first eight weeks a new employee is on the job can be as high as fifty percent. After eight weeks it's close to zero; like any business we lose employees to death and retirement and sickness and changing family needs. But, unlike many businesses, we rarely lose people to dissatisfaction in any guise. One result is that our competitors know that raiding the company for talent is pretty futile and frustrating.

"'Dignity' is a three-legged stool: compensation, creativity, and involvement. We pay our people well, more than people in comparable jobs at other firms are paid, and our benefits are generous, including our profit-sharing plan.

"The second leg—creativity—is less obvious, less tangible, and less measurable: it goes by other, more descriptive names like 'stretching' or 'creative overload'."

I asked one employee why he signed on with Allegheny Financial right out of college: "I think that the overall reason was the future Jim and others painted for me. I was offered training to become a Certified Financial Planner—an important recognition of competency that is a prerequisite for success—and was told that I would be 'educated' i.e. work in each of the three areas of the company to gain a broad view of the entire business and how it functions as a cooperative organism.

"Perhaps most important, I was told that I would not be expected to contribute to revenue until after my education was complete in three to four years. Jim I know is convinced that impatience for financial results can be counterproductive in that it can actually lose customers with products and services that fall short of standards. In essence, the company promised me a second college experience and a solid foundation of knowledge before exposing me to clients.

"I stay here because Jim knows exactly when and how far to stretch me to expand my capabilities and keep me totally involved and interested in my job. For example, I immediately attended all sorts of meetings with clients and their accountants and lawyers, and I was put in charge of a limited partnership we formed, under Jim's wing, of course. That first partnership has been so successful that I was

asked to form a second along the same lines and purposes. I am now one of the three General Partners that manage a growing portfolio.

"The bottom line is that I can see my business life twenty, thirty years down the road, which has big advantages. I have a clear vision of my career path and what I need to do to be successful ... all of which is vital as I work toward a partnership.

To sum it up, I'm here for what the first President Bush called 'the vision thing'. The company and I share the same vision of my future, and we like what we see."

By the way, this person became, after twelve years with the firm, President of the planning group.

Jim Browne continued: "Involvement is also best explained by example. One long-standing client—who complains on the one hand that we over-service his modest account and on the other hand that he doesn't see enough of us because he enjoys our chats about our lives and the fresh insights he seems always to extract— is also a wine buff. He would object to 'connoisseur' as far too elevating and pompous, and in fact calls himself more of a wine snob. Anyway, he opens his house to me and the six others on my immediate staff—and that includes our receptionist—who help him be comfortable about his funds and life.

"He has told me repeatedly that managing his assets is only a small part of managing his comfort, his sense of well-being that allows him to focus on his own career and life and not on the inevitable ups and downs of the various financial markets. We gather twice a year or so for a lunch at his home that is really a reason for him to uncork and share his latest discoveries in his world of fine wines. My staff and I win with a clearer understanding of this client's thinking, a deeper empathy, if you will, of his needs that we can transfer, at least in part, to other clients. We all win with a good time."

The client responds: "When I retained Jim to manage my money I expected just that and no more. I underestimated him and his people right from the get-go of our relationship, when he asked me to answer some five pages of questions, in writing, about many other parts of my current life and how I envisioned my future. Answering those questions forced me to think more deeply and sensibly about what I was doing, and, perhaps more important, what I wanted to do down the road. Like many of us, I had vague notions about these things that I had not bothered to crystallize in any great detail, preferring to delude myself that I know on some intuitive level.

"'What make and model car do you drive?'" was one question that puzzled me. Sure, my car counts as an asset of sorts, and, from that point of view, its value enters into any calculation of my net worth.

"That's not what Jim had in mind. When we sat down to review my answers, he stared into my eyes and said: 'You must understand that you are your most important asset; nothing in your portfolio of stocks and bonds, even your total portfolio, earns as much as you do. Even if we discount your earning power, consider that without you there is no reason for your stocks and bonds. So I want you to sell your car and buy a safer model".

"Now, there's an unexpected leap of logic," I said.

"Not so," he replied. "Your car ranks among the least safe on the road," and he showed me the crash test results to prove it. He then gave me a list of safer cars and suggested that I work out a trade, which I did that week. Who could ignore advice like that?"

A Quiet, Revealing Conversation

Jim and his three assistants—Brandon, Carolyn, and Tara—met with me over lunch to discuss how their company fits within the framework and purpose of this book.

Brandon opened with some history: "Jim formed this team about five years ago, and selected us very carefully for our sensitivity to clients' needs. The absolute key personal characteristic he was looking for is our ability to listen, and we think it's key to what I can only describe as our phenomenal growth."

Jim added: "Pete, you've mentioned to me several times that the scarcest resource in business today is paying attention. We can't afford to <u>not</u> pay attention; we cannot plan and manage a client's finances unless we know that client, and I mean "know" in ways that are far broader and deeper than his or her money. For example, how much risk is tolerable and how much can be spent on so-called personal assets. Both are basic personality traits."

At this point I noticed that everyone at the table looked intently at whoever was speaking and didn't say a word, and I thought how different we are than the people on the talk shows and meetings at other companies during which interrupting and" talking over" are so prevalent and annoying. How could anybody possibly hear, much less understand, what was being said?

"Our number one priority" said Carolyn, "is to provide clients with a service they can't find anywhere else, service that exceeds simply planning and managing portfolios. We literally become involved in almost every facet of our clients' lives, creating long-term relationships based on mutual trust and respect.

"One recent example: we were one of six firms being considered to manage the significant holdings of a wealthy family. When we won the account, I asked why and was told that the other five companies came to the first meeting with contracts all filled in and ready to be signed, which this person thought was pretty presumptuous. We came in with a blank pad and pencil and asked the right, probing questions, and then listened to the answers. They recognized that we were there to learn, and then submit a proposal based on knowledge of their specific needs. We were the thoughtful supplier; our competitors the cookie cutter suppliers."

"Uncaring cookie cutters" interrupted Tara. "How can they care for a customer if they don't understand him or her? Impossible."

I chimed in. "I told you that you don't manage my money; you simplify my life by eliminating the chaos, the worries about my assets. I have much more time for myself now. I even gave up reading the *Wall Street Journal* for an hour every morning. My brain is clear of that kind of useless clutter."

"We want our clients to get more out of life, to do what they like to do and not fret over their money," added Brandon. "We simplify their lives in many ways, and maybe that's the key word: simplify. Look at your life, Pete. When you came here, almost ten years ago, you were collecting at least fifty pieces of paper a month on all sorts of far-flung investments and you struggled to calculate your net worth and found it impossible to calculate yields. Now, we synthesize all that for you, and you can concentrate on your career and hobbies."

"I never could understand that phrase, 'it's not personal; it's just business'" said Carolyn. "Our business is very personal; I put my personal touch to calls, emails, letters and so on, and our clients recognize and appreciate it. So the personal approach helps us grow in countless, intangible ways. On top of that, it's just plain more fun for everyone."

"Our fee structure enters into the picture too," said Jim. "We might charge a flat yearly retainer or a percentage of assets under management, never a per-hour that nickels and dimes. As a result, clients are much more comfortable calling us with their concerns or for advice. Not one has abused that simple perk. And we try, via a thorough review, to cut the taxes for each client by at least as much as our fee. In that way, our clients for all intents and purposes get our services for nothing.

"Here are a few examples. One client didn't realize that nursing home fees are tax deductible until we pointed that out to him. The savings were huge. We've lowered financing costs for several clients by restructuring debt, lowered medical insurance costs for another couple by pointing out that they were insuring their grown children who had their own policies, and another elderly couple who carried insurance for pregnancy when they were well beyond childbearing age."

Tara then pointed out services that are beyond the norm. "We found a deficiency in one client's liability coverage, and showed another how to provide for a disabled child after the client's death." Tara chuckled: "One client literally came back from the grave to ask us for a favor. His will stipulated that his funeral be a major bash at his club, that we handle all the arrangements, and that Jim give a speech about the many happy and upbeat times in the client's life that we shared and loved. This person wanted his friends to celebrate, not mourn."

"I was flattered and flabbergasted at the same time," said Jim.

"It was a task equal to planning a mid-size wedding," added Carolyn. "We pulled it off."

I thought back to when I sent my daughter to Jim for a consultation; she had just inherited about $40,000 and wanted to invest it prudently. This team did as thorough a life style analysis for her as they would have for a multi-million dollar account. And charged nothing. I'm sure that my daughter and her husband won't forget this extraordinary service and will become clients when the time is right.

"OK," I said to Jim's three assistants, "what about you guys. What keeps you working at Allegheny? Brandon has already talked about his clear career path and his abilities being stretched."

Carolyn answered: "If I'm going to spend eight, ten hours a day anywhere, I want to enjoy those hours. I do, and my attitude shows through to clients. To provide that higher level of service I mentioned earlier, you must enjoy giving it.

"I agree with Brandon about stretching; we're encouraged to think 'outside the box', to come up with good ideas to improve ourselves and the business, and implement them. Management is very receptive, very approachable to new ideas. And I don't want to neglect the high standards of integrity and ethics set by our managers and partners, and that we naturally follow. I sleep well because of that."

"Let's not forget money," added Tara. "We are all paid well, so more is expected of us, which adds to the 'stretch' idea. I think all of us agree that we could not leave here without taking a major cut in both psychic and monetary pay; I know I couldn't."

***

IN 2013, Jim Browne is sliding into retirement but still keeps on top of the planning and asset management segment of the business, acts as adviser to other employees, and manages a few key accounts. He has turned over responsibility for daily operations to Brandon Haynes, who earned his CFP and has been promoted to President of the segment at age 39. Carolyn Madigan has been named Partner and Practice Manager with extensive responsibilities managing customer satisfaction, and Tara Miller has greatly broadened her responsibilities to include tracking the several hedge funds in which the company's customers are invested.

"We're basically the same company we were in 2004, except bigger" noted Brandon."We now employ 1.5 times more people and they manage twice the assets for twice the number of customers. We moved to bigger offices to house our larger staff, we're still looking for people who adhere to and believe in our ways of doing business, and we're still treating employees and customers with the dignity they deserve. As a result, our turnover rate of employees—after they've been on board for eight weeks-- and customers is still so low that we don't bother to measure it; we just know that it is below two percent."

6. THE BARTENDER AS ENTREPRENEUR

THE SWEETEST WORDS ARE A PERSON'S NAME, WELCOME BACK, AND 'THE SAME'.

IN 2004, I met Frank while attending a convention in D.C. Around three o'clock one slow afternoon I strolled into his bar (and "his" is the right word, as you'll see) in the small and upscale hotel in which I was staying, papers to be studied under my arm and a deep need for a stiff drink in my eyes. Frank—thin, trim, dressed in the traditional royal-red Eisenhower jacket over a starched white shirt and black bow tie—stopped polishing his wine glasses, already glistening, and asked me my pleasure. "Vodka mart, rocks, dry, no fruit," I recited, as I slid onto a cushioned bar stool and glanced at the few fellow afternoon drinkers and an expensive lounge that I'd love to call my living room.

Our chat covered the usual idle banter that's endemic in most bars: Pittsburgh and why so many people think of it as bigger and dirtier than it is, what's right and wrong with the Steelers and Redskins, what I do for a living, how long he had been at his bar (decades, it turns out), why I was in D.C., our kids—and so on.

But—I felt a big difference that told me that this was no ordinary barkeep. I realized that Frank really listened (paying attention is probably the rarest skill in business today, yet it can pay off handsomely, as was discussed in Chapter 5). He was really interested, and I found myself really listening and becoming interested in him; amazing how it always works that way. (Try it with your boss, significant other, and friends and reap the benefits.) Over two hours, we developed the kind of underlying rapport that I had experienced only with long-standing friends.

Or long-standing clients.

I returned to D.C. two years later for another version of the same convention, and I made it a point to stay in that same hotel. I again walked into the bar one slow afternoon. "Hi, Pete," Frank greeted me, "welcome back. The usual?" and he made me my mart, rocks, dry, no fruit. We picked up our conversation as if we had never ended it, and I marveled that we did. After all, we both had met and talked with literally thousands of people since we had last met.

Studies show that sales reps in places like department stores—and, presumably bars and restaurants—who remember customers' names increase sales 239 percent over reps who do not remember customers' names. A touch on the arm can increase sales even more.

The story hasn't ended. Some four years later I went to D.C. to an opera, and didn't think even once about booking another hotel even though my travel agent said that Frank's Place isn't at all convenient to the opera theater at Kennedy Center. Frank wasn't behind the bar—he died a year before, the new bartender told me. "But," he said, "he's here"—and he pointed to a brass plaque, 'Frank's Bar', prominently on the back wall. I told the interloper my story, and he chuckled: "I've heard dozens of stories like that, no two exactly alike. Frank recruited an army of friends who came back here time and time again. He treated customers like they should and want to be treated, and—you wanna know something strange in today's world?—the hotel's managers knew it and counted up all that repeat business and treated him like a king. On top of that, they treat all of us like kings and queens, hoping to make us all Franks. This is the best hotel to work in anywhere, I'd guess, and it's all because of Frank."

My lady friend and I decided to dine that evening at the hotel restaurant, partly because it had recently been voted 'most romantic dining spot' and partly because I wanted to learn more about Frank. What was it about him that compelled people, like me, who know dozens of bartenders, to return time and again not only to his bar, but also to the hotel?

My waiter listened quietly to my little story of crossing paths with Frank, and, without saying a word, disappeared into the kitchen and returned with the chef.

"Frank is the reason I'm here," the chef said after we were introduced. I asked for the story, and he sat down, suggested dinner and the right wine. "On the house," he said. "We'll celebrate his life."

"Frank had an amazing charisma, an amazing memory, and the two are inseparable," he said. "He never forgot a name or face or the story behind it. A mind like that—he could have been a chess champion.

"Anyway, he called me about five years ago and asked if I'd join him here. Told me he'd built a large group of steady customers who really appreciate fine dining and service. By that time his reputation was everywhere, so I agreed. Frank convinced the hotel's managers that we'd make a terrific team, and we did. This small dining room"—and he swung his arms in a wide circle that took in all twenty, thirty tables—"can't be beat for its friendliness, and, I like to think, for its fine food and drink. Business has been very good—profitable, and enjoyable, too, for us and for our customers."

I reflected on the drive back to Pittsburgh that Frank was a marvelous businessman; he intuitively understood the win-win behind successful relationships, and was willing to make the effort to form and keep them. He won with a decades-long career that I'm sure paid handsomely in tips and friendships. His employers at the hotel won with an extraordinary amount of repeat business—I was the perfect example, and I was only one of hundreds, maybe thousands-- not only for the bar and dining room, but also for rooms. Congratulations of the highest order to the managers of the hotel for recognizing Frank's contributions to the entire business. And other employees won with a role model who literally created-- single-handedly-- a great place to work that probably would be just another hotel if he had never been there. Quite a legacy.

There Are Other Franks in the World

Back in Pittsburgh I thought about the many bartenders and restaurant owners I know, and why I return gleefully and often to some and not to others. I feel unusually well-qualified to talk about this because I am somewhat of a social gadabout and am recognizable in the small cultural district of this small city.

Mark, an imposing figure behind the semi-circular bar of an upscale restaurant in which he owns a piece, always greets me with "Hi Pete, wine or scotch tonight? What show did you see? Anything good?" and then, "I see that Duke is hot on the boards again this year. You'll be watching a lot of basketball." I see Mark at least twice a week, and his bar is usually packed two and three deep with people who are treated with the same jovial friendliness as I am.

John, around the corner at an equally upscale restaurant, always greets me with that tired, generic "What'll it be?" I asked him once why he doesn't address me by name; after all, I know his. His reply: "I'm good at remembering faces, not names." I see John maybe once a month, despite being almost always able to get a seat at his bar. Not surprising, eh?

Craig owns the hottest jazz joint in town, and it's only a ten-minute walk from my house. He—and his wife, Melissa, who works there off and on—<u>always</u> greet me by name, welcome me back, ask about my daughter in New York (where their son lives), when I'll be teaching again at Carnegie Mellon University (where their son was one of my students). Meanwhile, the bartendress, who has been there for many years, has, without anyone saying a word, poured me a glass of my favorite wine and is warming it in her hands because she knows I like it with the chill off. And she always delivers it with "Here Pete, enjoy." It's not surprising that I hear a lot of jazz at Craig's place, and so do many other people who also enjoy his camaraderie. As I've said, it's one of the hottest spots in town.

Joe is manager of a local restaurant that is part of a small chain. He always greets me by name and asks if I want my usual wine, or if I want to try a new variety. His bartendresses and waitresses know not only me by name, but also the names of the several clients and friends who regularly join me there for lunch. In a neighborhood packed with restaurants, I go to Joe's most often.

Am I a sucker for friendliness that I know is offered for some commercial gain but I'm sure is sincere, too? You bet I am, and I love it. Don't we all?

And for you who think that what I've discussed in this chapter is "conventional wisdom", I ask: If it's so conventional, why is it so rare? And is it applicable to every business? You bet it is.

**

IN 2013: Several years after I wrote Frank's story I returned to his bar and hotel, again with my lady friend. The head waitress recognized a couple in love, and steered us to the romance table in a secluded corner of the room. Our waitress, unprompted, I think, told us Frank's story, and I told her that I was part of it. She joined us at our table and e chatted for several minutes and toasted his memory. Maybe dignity endures; maybe it is the stuff of legacy.

7. CEC. THE HOW AND WHY OF PROFITABLE GROWTH IN A FLAT MARKET

EXTRAORDINARY EMPATHY FOR CUSTOMERS AND EMPLOYEES IS KEY TO THE RAPID GROWTH AND STELLAR REPUTATION OF CIVIL AND ENVIRONMENTAL CONSULTANTS.

IN 2004: "I want to start with some history, and how it led to how we manage our business," said Jim Nairn, one of the founders of CEC. "When we opened our doors, in April 1989, my three partners and I knew that our first responsibility to ourselves and to any of the employees we hoped to have down the road was to grow, the second to assure that employees, not outsiders, own the company. We were young, in our late thirties and forties, and had

92

been employed by other consulting firms; we knew the opportunities and pitfalls. We knew then, and know now, that only growth opens new opportunities for employees—the opportunities of new challenges that encourage creativity and entrepreneurism, that keep us fresh.

"In our formative years we were growing so fast—if you looked at growth on a percentage basis—that we were doubling the number of employees every few weeks. Of course the rate of growth has slowed as we've become larger; nevertheless, we've been named as one of Western Pennsylvania's fastest growing companies by the *Pittsburgh Business Times*.

"We grew despite being in stagnant markets. The reasons for our growth are quite basic. First, we know that our best customers now are our best customers in the future; we depend on them not only for repeat business, an increasingly larger share of their total business when that's possible, and for referrals to other companies that can use our services. In that way, we are a bit like a stockbroker who wants to manage as much of each client's money as the client is comfortable having him manage, and to refer him to other clients.

"Second, we are proactive marketers, never aggressive, in that we keep up with new and changing environmental regulations, allowing us to suggest studies and remediation to our customers. Our suggestions demonstrate quietly that we're on top of the business and on top of customers' needs...an important marketing tool that has paid off.

"I think an important consideration for growth is our approach to marketing. We employ one marketing person here, another in our Columbus branch—a very small staff for a company our size. They're responsible for things like brochures and press releases, rarely if ever for direct contact with potential new customers.

"Our project managers bear the larger burden of marketing. They are responsible for repeat business, and their bonuses reflect how successful they are in booking it. The result is that best of all worlds: a quality job delivered on time and within budget. In other words, a satisfied customer who wants to return often."

The engineers to whom I teach writing invariably think that 'sell' is the purpose of proposals, and 'inform' the purpose of reports. They're right about proposals, wrong about reports since reports are the bridge to the next contract. A poor report—one that is murky, incomplete, or not reflective of the intelligence that went into the project—is far less likely than a good report—one that is clear, concise, complete, and reflective of an understanding of the client's needs. Good project managers know that the primary purpose of both documents is to persuade, the secondary to inform.

Jim continued: "Third, we understand that our competitors come and go in this business, and, when one goes for whatever reason, we might look upon its misfortune as our opportunity. We could take over its clients—by the way, we never raid another company's clients or employees, and expect the same courtesies from them. Nevertheless, their clients need a new supplier, and, if conditions are right, we offer our services. We also use the collapse of a company to broaden our range of services and expertise in a market niche in which we weren't a player, plus customers needing those specialized services. Employees and customers win with continuity, and we win with growth.

"The other and ugly side of growth is stagnation, which is deadly for the company and its employees. It's the curse of something else having gone wrong, and the result is almost always the curse of disgruntled employees and customers, followed by high turnover of both. What an expensive curse that is! The cost of hiring new employees is phenomenal, as everyone in business knows. The initial cost is high enough, but, frankly, it's small compared to having an employee on board who doesn't fit the culture. We've been fortunate to avoid that more often than not. And the cost of finding a new customer to replace one we've lost for whatever reason is at least ten times the cost of keeping one. Again, we've been fortunate, and have lost very few customers after almost thirty years in business—more about that later—and almost all our new business stems from customers who we're either doing work for now or have worked for in the past."

Jim laced the fingers of his hands, then continued: "Given that broad vision of growth, we've adopted three major, very related, and equally important strategies—I'd be hard-pressed to place one as more important than the other: Customers who subscribe to our culture, the best employees who want to stay and build careers, and an orderly transition of ownership.

* * * *

"Come to our company's picnics and other informal events and you'll see many of us wearing t-shirts that shout "Client Focus." It's more than a slogan here; we like to think of it as a way of life that is nurtured by how we're organized and operate.

"I suppose that our guiding principle and privilege is to give each client more than expected, more than we promised, and every time I say or think that I'm reminded of the local butcher shop in my neighborhood. He stays in business despite the supermarket around the corner simply because he greets his customers by name and suggests a cut that fits their taste. He offers a personal touch that the supermarket abandoned long ago, but which many people still appreciate and are willing to pay a bit extra to enjoy.

"We give more than expected in a number of ways. Our senior managers, for example are involved in some way in every project, sometimes at the request of the client, more often to demonstrate our confidence in our project manager and to transfer responsibility to him or her. That transfer, by the way is important: it's one way our employees grow into more responsible jobs and become more valuable to themselves and to the company.

"Our project managers are doers more than managers; I suppose the buzzword is 'hands-on'. They are responsible for every detail of the project and are evaluated and their bonuses paid by the satisfaction of customers as measured by anecdotal evidence and the hard data of repeat business".

Jerry Dettore was the deputy executive director Pittsburgh's Urban Redevelopment Authority. "My staff and I have worked continuously with CEC, especially when we were so deeply involved with a number of brownfield projects during which we are always running into new challenges. CEC was quick to estimate the cost of the work, always conservatively; they rarely exceed their estimate, saving me the many headaches of going back to my board for more money and explaining why. Several other suppliers tend to lowball costs to get the job, then 'make it up' with the extras. That always creates problems with budgets, and it almost always delays completion of the work.

"As a public agency, we are required to solicit bids for work and to award contracts to a broad range of suppliers. We try to work as much as possible with CEC and it's easy to understand why. Perhaps it's a cliché to say this, but it's true: I can depend on them to think outside the box and come up with creative solutions. In short, CEC is the premier environmental consultant in this area, and they've earned our support."

"The success of our client focus is summed up by one early case study. About fifteen years ago we lost a client, and I hesitate to use 'lost', because the situation was so peculiar. We were in charge of vacuuming the soil out from around some storage tanks at a plant owned by a large chemical company; another company, selected by the client, was in charge of cleaning the soil, using bacteria that ate and digested the pollutants. Well, the cleaning process didn't work as planned, and we ended up with mounds of smelly soil, some very unhappy neighbors, and an emergency. We needed to change the course of this remediation project.

"My repeated and urgent calls to the client's vice president in charge weren't answered, so, as a last recourse, I emailed their project manager. That got the vice president's attention, all right. "You'll never work for us again," he said. Why? Because I put the situation in writing, leaving a trail for future litigation.

"The client was true to his word: he's never called us in to bid on a project. I reciprocated by never asking him to. His management style is the antithesis of ours, and we don't need that kind of cultural tension. Did we lose a client, or did the client lose a supplier?"

"I was a client who became a supplier," laughed Dan Swed. "For many years I was director of environmental affairs at Armco Steel, where my department was staffed to handle the normal workload. When we were overloaded I called in outside consultants such as CEC. Over the years, CEC's project people and I developed strong friendships based on mutual respect.

"In May 1999 Armco was purchased by Kawasaki Steel, AK Steel was formed, and I was suddenly one of two directors of environmental affairs. I found myself on the cusp of being 'redundant' and on the

street, especially now that I was with a company infamous for the undignified practice of cutting heads at the slightest dip in sales or profits.

"Jim Nairn called an hour after the acquisition was announced and asked if I would be interested in joining CEC as a vice president and part owner. I was flattered, of course, and also curious about what I would bring to Jim's party. After all, I reasoned, I had never been a consultant unless I thought of myself as an 'internal consultant', and I was management oriented, not task oriented as I know consultants must be.

"Jim explained that I would bring a customer's perspective, a kind of insider's insight, to the business, and that would be very valuable. He went further to say that my expertise in resolving the environmental problems of the steel and other metals businesses could expand that market niche for CEC, which fits the company's strategies for growth.

"I've been here for more than ten years, and, I suppose because my experience as a customer is so ingrained, I still wonder if I'm a credible consultant. My friends and peers tell me that I'm the only person who does."

Jim continued: "Good people stick with us for very good reasons. We think of our people—and our people think of themselves—as spokes in a wheel. Each spoke is essential if the wagon is to move; if one spoke breaks, the wheel and the wagon collapse, useless. It's our metaphor for teamwork, and it's our reason to treat employees as the valuable contributors they are.

"CEC provides substantial and generous benefits to all employees: health insurance, including coverage for prescription drugs; disability and life insurance; a matching 401(k) that is vested from day one of employment, which is very rare; a bonus plan that involves everybody from the janitor to the CEO; and tuition refunds for continuous learning. We then go the extra mile with our employee assistance plan—and with our employee stock ownership plan, both of which are worth discussing further.

"I think that our employee assistance plan is so different from anything I've heard of in business that I can get away with calling it 'unique'. Basically, we help employees and their families cope with all types of problems that affect their personal lives or job performance, and we do it without charge. In effect, what we do with the program is spread the costs of extraordinary misfortune among all our employees.

"Some quick examples: An engineer who contracted Lou Gehrig's disease was kept on the job as long as he—not managers—felt he could perform. When he decided he couldn't, CEC sent him and his family to the Caribbean for a long vacation.

"CEC paid the salary of a technician who developed breast cancer during that period when short-term disability insurance ran out and long-term disability kicked in.

"And when the wife of one of our engineers in our Atlanta office gave birth to a severely deformed child who needs a series of very expensive operations, we paid what insurance didn't cover, a tidy sum. Then, when the couple wanted to move back to Pittsburgh, the four founders met to discuss the situation. One asked: "If the child were not in the picture, would we move them back?" The answer was a unanimous yes, and we did.

"What's the headline about CEC from your point of view?" I was chatting with Marlene Harbert, human resources manager.

"Easy question," she replied. "The worst day here is better than the best day working anywhere else."

"Powerful stuff, especially coming from an HR pro. Tell me more."

"I'll never forget my two interviews to get this job, in 1999. Both were with the four founders. I could feel the camaraderie, the respect, the healthy joy of being here. We actually laughed almost

the entire few hours we were together. I went home after the second interview and told my husband that I feel compelled to work for these guys. I figured that they treated employees that same way they treated each other. I was right."

"Do other employees feel the same way?"

"Judging by our turnover rate, I'd say so. Our rate is so low that we don't even measure it. I could if I had to, but what's the point? And, by the way, many of our employees have been with the company since its founding,; the core of our genesis is still on board.

"Low turnover is great for growth, a connection that can be obscure to many managers. Say we lose an employee, a project manager. It costs at least three times that employee's salary to replace him or her, probably much more if you consider the loss of continuity with the customer followed by the potential loss of repeat business. We also lose the respect of others in the industry—believe me, the word gets around when an employee leaves, and that can make it more difficult to hire new people."

"So you go the extra mile to keep your people?"

"Absolutely. Great benefits, as Jim has said, flexible hours and policies, and stability that's almost unheard of in consulting—we've rarely laid off a soul. Our base salaries are competitive and can grow by up to twenty percent with incentives for performance."

"How do you measure performance?"

"We look at the company's profits and divvy them out; that's the short-term measure and it's used to calculate only twenty percent of the total. The remaining eighty percent is based on 'professional growth', because it can be marketed to customers over the long term. We examine such factors as personal goals set each year, were the goals met, continuous learning, expansion of skills...the things that clients look for when they select a consultant. Our incentives encourage employees to be with us happily throughout their careers, which is indicative of our management focus."

* * * *

Jim added: "I'm convinced that employees who own a piece of the action work more diligently toward growing the business than employees who don't have a stake. I suppose that that's conventional wisdom that bears repeating only because it's so important. I'm also convinced that it would be terribly selfish of the four founders, all in our fifties and sixties, to not transfer ownership to the next generation. As a result, all of our employees from assistant manager up are eligible to participate in our stock ownership plan, which we started in the late nineties. Now, about half the company is owned by employees, and that percentage is growing every month as they buy more with automatic withdrawals from their paychecks, and the company's matching funds. Some of our people now own three, four percent of the company, which is valued well into six figures. . The stock, by the way, kept increasing in value during the general market downturns during 2000-2003 and 2006--2007.

"The opposite side of the ownership coin is that managing for stockholder value and selling stock in the company to outsiders isn't for us. Our growth by way of retaining good employees who are proud of their quality work that is completed on time and within budget, and customers who understand that that is the antithesis of what Wall Street wants and cares about: numbers, not people. So we decided, almost from the first days we were in business, to not go public. Besides, I honestly don't think that the consulting business fits the profile of a public company. The ROI can be impressive because the 'I' is so low, but the ROS tends to be far lower.

"I wish I could find a more descriptive word than "relationship" to describe our extraordinary closeness to customers and employees. Perhaps '"affinity" would be better. Or "amalgamation", or "camaraderie". Regardless of its label, we assign a very high value to the concept, and it's working. We're still growing robustly, and our employee and customer turnover rates are low. I don't find it at all surprising that our hiring and marketing costs are very low as well."

**

IN 2013: The firm has more than doubled its workforce and revenues, and profitability is acceptable and realistic for the industry. Services are now offered throughout the United States from 16 branch offices, and still other branches are being considered, a prime testament to the firm's business model. Jim Nairn has relinquished the presidency and devotes his time to such strategic endeavors as managing key customers and locating new offices. And virtually all employees are stockholders, intensifying incentives to create and keep customers and to minimize turnover.

The firm plans to continue growing: The HR manager and his staff of five are searching for some 50 new employees—almost a ten-percent increase in total employment--and are training office mangers to be results-oriented hirers and trainers.

8. IT'S ALL ABOUT PEOPLE!

THIS HIGH-TECH FIRM HAS BEEN GROWING AT SIXTY PERCENT/YEAR BY LIVING CORE VALUES THAT CENTER ON PEOPLE, AND THAT NEVER MENTION REVENUE OR PROFIT.

The notion that growth of revenue and profit is the result of employee and customer satisfaction is clearly and unmistakably reflected in Vocollect Engineering, the global leader in voice-directed distribution.

"Management is all about people", said Roger Byford, chief technology officer, chairman, and one of the two founders of this high-tech firm. "Our core purpose is to create opportunity for all of us to grow and excel in a fun and rewarding environment. That purpose stems from my past, and the past of our other founder, and protects our employees from falling into the same situation. We were both research scientists for a huge conglomerate, assigned to develop voice technology—the use of voice to enter data into a computer for such purposes as inventory control and other functions in warehouses. The commercial possibilities of the technology were too small for management to pay much attention to it or to fund it adequately. So my partner and I found ourselves in frustrating, dead-end jobs that we learned to dislike intensely. We wanted jobs without ceilings on our creativity and resourcefulness, and we wanted to offer similar jobs to others with similar feelings; we started Vocollect.

"Our five core values support the core purpose, and are replete with such words as 'utmost integrity...team-oriented...friendly...individual initiative...creativity...intelligence... balancing personal and professional lives...and do the right thing for each other and for our customers."

"What about growth of revenue and profits?" I asked. Financial growth is important, of course, but isn't mentioned simply because it's a byproduct of good management, and, as I mentioned earlier, good management is all about people. Nevertheless, it's fundamental that no business can survive without the financial results that

gladden the hearts of investors, but there's more to it than that. Growth also keeps employees happy by opening new opportunities to move to the next technical or commercial challenge—to develop the next generation of products that customers need, for example-- or to move to the next rung up on the corporate ladder that wouldn't open up otherwise, and so on. The bottom line is that we owe it to our employees and customers to grow so that they can."

"Several contributors to this book have talked about the importance of 'integrity' and 'do the right thing', which are pretty abstract concepts. How do you define them, and how do you know that everyone in your organization lives them?"

"Integrity is, simply, it is what it is, or what you see and hear is real. I could expand that by stating that you never want to do something that you wouldn't want to hear at your own funeral. That cliché encompasses honesty and much more, such as decency, trustworthiness, soundness, a certain openness that is reflected by a willingness to bare our business souls when appropriate.

"Here's an example: Our salespeople work directly with companies that operate their own warehouses, such as Wal-Mart and many of the grocery chains; they're the end-users of our products and services. They also work with companies that we call our 'partners', for example companies that sell material handling equipment to the same end users. We want our partners to sell us as part of their package without feeling that we might go directly to the end-users, so we pay our salespeople the same commission for either type of sale, and we make sure that our partners know it. Our openness has worked: partners now account for sixty percent of our revenue, up from zero only six years ago."

"Let's talk about employees. What's your turnover rate, and why?"

Roger thought for a minute or two: "I can't remember when an engineer—the people for whom I am directly responsible as chief technology officer-- has left us, and we now employ seventy of them. And I don't remember anyone else leaving us either, regardless of responsibility or job title. Turnover rate is so low, close to zero across the company, that we don't track it. However, I'm not considering the occasional mis-hire who leaves, or is asked to leave, usually after only ninety days or so on the job. We've made a few mistakes on the front end of an employee's tenure and, when we realize that we have, we try very hard to find the right slot for that person. Sometimes we succeed, sometimes we don't.

"We revel in the benefits of low-to-no turnover-- the far lower costs of hiring and training that are reflected directly on the bottom line, and the added time that we can devote to improving the business. We spend more time doing what we like to do and do best.

"Why is our turnover rate so low? Because we live by our core purpose and values every day and in every way imaginable."

"I see a huge need for communicating with employees and customers."

"Communicating with each other was easy when there were only a few of us; we all knew what we needed to know to function as an efficient organization with a defined mission simply by talking to each other and writing the occasional memo. Once we had more than twenty employees—looking back, it seems that twenty is the cutoff point—communications became a big problem, not because we didn't communicate enough, but because we communicated too much. Email has made it too easy to transcend the barriers of 'need to know' to 'send it anyway to be sure all the bases are covered'. I'm sure that many organizations are afflicted with a similar overload.

"One of my current challenges, now that we employ more than two hundred people, is to find a way to slow down or prevent over communicating, which might require more communicating to employees to alert them of the situation—a Catch 22?-- and to consider readers' needs more carefully.

"Clear and concise communications serve another purpose that we consider very important: they tend to stop political bickering, the backbiting and jockeying for position with the brass that I found so prevalent and distasteful with my previous employer. When everybody knows where everybody else stands, there's no need for this type of destructive behavior.

"As for our end-user and partner customers—there are more than one hundred customer companies, no two exactly alike, and many more people within those companies—a core value is, again, 'do the right thing'. One right thing is to communicate with them on all levels, from top management to the folks on the warehouse floor who use our hardware and software.

"We keep in touch with customers via the usual personal visits, attending their trade shows, and advertising in their magazines. For example, we attend trade shows specifically for the grocery business, and advertise in Super Market news, among other magazines."

"Have you ever lost a customer?"

"Well, that depends on what you mean by 'lost'". We don't win every contract we bid on; it's unrealistic to expect to. In fact, we plan to win one out of three: one of the other two is cancelled, and the other is awarded to a competitor. Our hit rate is actually much higher, so our projections are conservative.

"But, we've never lost a customer once we've started to work. I guess that's a customer satisfaction rate of one hundred percent, and I'm proud of that. In that same vein, I'm very proud that many of our customers extend our original contract to other warehouses. For example, we are Wal-Mart's sole supplier of warehouse inventory systems—throughout the world. That's a particularly important achievement given Wal-Mart's well-known standards for efficiency and excellence for everything it buys."

"If I can summarize a bit, one reason that employees and customers are loyal to you is your core values. There must be others."

"Studies show that employees everywhere are loyal because of such characteristics of the organization as providing opportunities to do their best work and to grow into new responsibilities, recognition and respect for performance, knowing what's expected, and others that are fundamental to self-actualization and, in turn, happiness. I also believe that good managers encourage people, first, to build on their strengths, and, at a distant second, to strengthen their weaknesses. To that latter point, I feel that we in business devote too much time and effort trying to fix what doesn't need to be fixed, or can be improved only marginally.

"We also play the 'stick and carrot' game, if you'll excuse me for reversing the cliché. The stick in my mind is the here and now. Our pay scale is certainly competitive in our industry and geographic area. Bonuses can add an unlimited sum to any employee's base pay, and are paid for performance of the individual, the team on which the individual works, and the company as a whole. Goals for performance are set by the individual and his or her boss, that boss's boss, and up the ladder so that we are all complementing and not duplicating each other, so that we're all working toward the same result.

"The carrot is the future. Our 401K is generous; the company contributes fifty percent of employees' contributions of up to six percent of total pay. And every employee is given, at no cost, stock options that could lead to a hefty payday should we ever go public, or if we are ever acquired or merged into a public company."

"A recurring theme throughout this book, one that you mention in your core purpose, is the need to create a fun environment. How do you go about creating one?"

"Fun to me is doing what I enjoy doing—I think that's a universal definition-- and I want everyone here to do just that. I have a selfish reason, of course-- I know that people who enjoy their working hours are more dedicated, enthusiastic, resourceful, and creative—all those good qualities that all managers look for in all employees.

"I set the example for fun in 2001 when I was CEO and hated the job; I'm far more comfortable and competent working as a technologist than as a manager. I convinced our board to search for and hire a professional manager. He has worked out very well, and I'm more focused on working with our engineers to improve our existing products and expand their applications. The other founder took a similar path; a research engineer at heart, he elected to not accept a top manager's job to be vice president of new product development.

"Changing jobs to be happier isn't exclusively for those at the top of the organization. A plant engineer was recently promoted to head of production and found that he wasn't comfortable with the added responsibilities and wanted his former job back. He got it."

"Aren't you talking about freedom here? The freedom to move within the company, to discuss hopes and aspirations with top managers and be heard?"

"Yes, and freedom doesn't stop there. We don't have a vacation policy, for example. Instead, we give 'off days'—eighteen of them for new employees, more for veterans. Employees can take them whenever they want, and use them however they want—sick days, vacation days, whatever. Managers never need to wonder if an employee calling in sick, for example, really is; it's the employee's responsibility and choice"

"How would you summarize your success and the reasons for it?"

"We had three employees, including the two founders, in 1987 when Vocollect got off the ground. We now have more than two hundred employees and will hire another forty to fifty this year. We do more business in a week than we did all year only six years ago and the pipeline for new business is full, even overflowing. Our employees and customers are loyal; people want to work here, and customers want to work with us. I just handed out pretty hefty bonus checks for last year. In short, we're enjoying our success; we're having fun.

"Why? Our core purpose and values are all about people. Simple."

IN 2013, Vocollect is now a business unit of Intermec, Inc, and has opened several new offices worldwide and in the Pittsburgh area, and has formed relationships with several other firms such as

Honeywell ... all of which leads me to believe that the firm has grown and prospered at a phenomenal rate.On the negative side of this story, I tried and failed several times to call Roger for an update, so I have no idea where he is or what he's doing.

9. THE AUTHOR AS GLOBAL CONGLOMERATE

WHERE MAKE 'EM SMILE IS THE OVERARCHING IMPERATIVE.

IN 2004: I admit to being addicted to managing for Dignity simply because it has worked well.

I usually describe Geissler, Inc., of which I am president and also am privileged to brew the coffee and mix the martinis, as 1.5 people who are in the cerebral business, confusing everyone within earshot. In fact, my core business is writing speeches, articles, marketing stuff of all types, and strategies for businesses. What I do is very cerebral indeed since I help my clients think via writing. Yes, one of the more important reasons to write is to cleanse thinking, a thought expressed years ago by any number of writers such as Henry Miller, who said, "Writing, like life itself, is a voyage of discovery."

My corporation (aka me), on top of writing for business, is into teaching writing at the university graduate level and at companies and associations, turning out a book now and then, and occasionally behaving as an advertising/public relations agency and marketing consultant. So I am a mini conglomerate that operates under the umbrella of "words and thinking that work," and I am global, with clients, by way of clients in my headquarters city, in Europe and the Far East.

I developed and honed—in the most casual, informal, and serendipitous way imaginable—overarching "strategies" (really principles, or value systems) during my first few years in business. Each is founded on observations of similar businesses, some with dozens of employees and customers; I subconsciously separated what seems to work and what doesn't. My single criterion for 'work' was subjective: employees and customers were enjoying themselves so much that they wanted to be together to help each other, the classic win-win that has been replaced too often by 'I win, you lose'. A correlation is that employees and customers stayed with the firm as if glued, and they smiled! I decided then and there that smiles are both the drivers and manifestations of success, and I wanted to surround myself with them.

I've used the words casual, subjective, and serendipitous for good reasons. I didn't decide consciously to observe other firms; I just did in the normal course of events, and I didn't decide that I needed a formal mission statement; I just created one in my head as I learned what works and doesn't. Many peers, competitors and other entrepreneurs ask me how I've managed to stay and thrive in this turnstile business for more than 30 years. I tend to reply that I wish I had planned it, for then I would be The Master Planner of all time. But I didn't plan it in the classic sense, of course, and the big corporations I work with would laugh at my informal planning process. Come to think of it, maybe they'd do themselves and others a big favor by emulating it. Regardless, serendipity and just plain good fortune played the biggest roles.

Anyway, the notion that smiles are the top line of my personal balance sheet and operating statement trickled down quite logically to my three strategies, all of which, again, are better described as principles.

1. *Stick to my knitting*—writing for other businesses and teaching—because I love it, and I won't be distracted by so-called support functions that I dislike and can't do well or quickly anyway. Doing so, of course, trades my billable hours for someone else's, a trade that I make gladly. So, as a first step, I retained a good and

trustworthy accountant and put him in charge of tracking (not critiquing) my annual—never monthly or quarterly—income and outgo, and filling out the countless forms demanded by the various levels of government with which corporations contend. I paid him a reasonable fee without qualms or grumbling.

My first accountant retired after being with me for 12 mutually beneficial years, surely not because the fees I paid him somehow made him rich. I retained another based on the first's recommendation, and he is still, more than fifteen years later, happily toting up my numbers and assuring that I don't fall into the clutches of the IRS. Each has asked me once if I wouldn't be able to run my business better if I had a monthly operating statement. "Nope," I answered, "because I have a good feel of how well I'm doing financially, and a feel is good enough. I don't want to manage by the numbers or on a short-term string."

My second step to activate this strategy was to hire an assistant to, mainly, process the words that I scribble on a lined tablet so that my clients can read them, and to understand my business in enough detail to answer questions from clients when I'm not handy. My first assistant was experienced in the business and stayed with me for eighteen years; my second, who knew nothing about the business but who is very bright and willing to learn,

121

stayed with me for eleven years. Each left reluctantly to pursue other interests, and each left richer than they ever thought they'd be simply because of strategy #3.

2. ***I'm for more rapport.*** I keep customers who appreciate my talents, and, if perchance I get involved with those who don't or can't, drop them as early in our relationship as possible, and as amicably—I am acutely sensitive about burning bridges.

Four individuals made up my customer base: three are marketing or other managers of various divisions within large companies; the fourth is a vice president of sales for a smaller firm. All are steady sources of work. A half-dozen or so other individuals became my 'peripheral' customers; all can be counted on for sporadic orders.

All have been working with me for more than 25 years, regardless of corporate restructurings, new job functions and titles, moves to other companies, recessions, and booms. In this age of shifting loyalties, "why?" is a legitimate question.

My professionalism and talents enter into the answer, of course, the fact that I am good at what I do, but that should be discounted quite severely. Here's why:

I can point to competitors who are also good writers and who struggle to retain clients and keep their doors open. So other factors enter into the picture, and the first is what I call the no-hassle job; I do not ask my client for more information, for example, until I have first exhausted all other sources. I do not ask for feedback on, say, first drafts when I am quite unsure about direction, content, or style, which is extremely rare if I have done my homework up front.

A second factor is to always look for ways to maximize my clients' investments in one assignment (e.g. a speech) by suggesting ways to use similar ideas and words in another medium (e.g. a speech converted to an article or a press conference). One example: an article covering the design of a hull for a high-performance boat, published in a magazine read by engineers, was revised easily to fit a training program for the company's salespersons and distributors.

I read many years ago that it costs something like ten times as much to find and develop a new customer than it does to keep one in the fold. (Ken Lovorn, in Chapter 11, says that it costs nothing to keep a customer if employees do their jobs. Jim Nairn in Chapter 7, agrees that ten times more is pretty accurate.) I've come to think that ten times is far too low an estimate; fifty or even one hundred times seems far more realistic, so I go to heroic lengths to keep my customers in the corporate fold. Some examples: I loaned a customer who was going through a divorce that tied up his assets temporarily the tuition for his son's college. I took charge of the funeral arrangements for another client when his father died and he became too distraught to function. I joined a golf club so clients could play either with or without me. I loaned the money for a down payment on a home that one client wanted to buy, but, because of unusual circumstances, couldn't qualify for a mortgage. And so on.

These acts of friendship were the main reasons I became the busiest and most expensive writer of corporate gargle in town--at least that's what my clients said I was—and I jokingly said that I would move smoothly from 110 percent of capacity to 140 and hardly miss the sleep. I was, in truth, working myself to death, so I called a meeting with my Big Four to discuss how we could work together to smooth the ups and downs and level me off at a more reasonable pace. We decided on a system of communication within which I would signal them when I saw a downturn coming, and they would postpone or accelerate certain assignments to accommodate me. That I am still alive is proof enough that it all worked pretty well for years, and not one of my clients jumped my ship for another.

But I think that there's a more important lesson to be learned: that rapport with clients works in all directions for the benefit of all. One client tells me often that he works with me because I am as interested in his success as I am in my own. Of course I am; his success means repeat business.

3. *Share the profits and benefits with employees and customers.* My formal profit-sharing plan for employees is extremely generous, and it's only one perk. I paid for the complete college education of my first assistant, and for all sorts of computer-skills courses for my second. The corporation pays all costs for health insurance and co-payments up to $50,000, and has made several interest-free loans to employees buying a home or car.

I am, as I write this, paying for the college education of my second assistant, and she has not worked steadily for me for several years. I'm doing this for both altruistic and selfish reasons: she is extremely intelligent and talented and I enjoy giving her the opportunity to develop her full potential. And I know that she compliments and thanks me to others whenever she can, and eventually that comes back in the form of psychic or financial rewards.

Customers share the profits—now, isn't THAT a novel idea—with free parking for baseball and football games (my home/office is near the stadiums), parties before and after the games, an invitation to the Geissler Invitational—billed as the world's most exclusive golf tournament since only twelve people are invited—and, perhaps most important for everyone concerned, a conference room for meetings not only with me, but also with their other suppliers. "Other suppliers" can include my competent and friendly competitors, and they—and my customers—ask regularly why I allow this apparent intrusion. The first reason is that I win: I love my good competitors; they stimulate and grow the market for our services and we all benefit. Besides, we often partner on the same projects. I dislike my bad competitors for the opposite reasons.

Everyone involved enjoys meeting at my place, where we can turn off the phones and other distractions such as unwanted visitors. No distractions equal a tighter focus on the project at hand, a higher level of creativity, and better products, which of course translates to satisfied customers and repeat business.

And then there's the sheer comfort of it: my place is fully stocked with coffees, teas, nibbles, and the best booze in the city. Late afternoon meetings that stretch into cocktail hour and, occasionally, a simple dinner, are the norm, and, because they are at my place, I don't waste time, billable time at that, driving to the desert wasteland of a corporate office. The costs of booze and food are so miniscule compared to the billable hours I gain that I don't even account for them. Everybody wins, even my clients, who get to leave their offices and imperious bosses for a legitimate reason.

The worst businessman I know is another writer of corporate information, and a pretty good one at that. Nevertheless, during his twenty-plus years in the business he has lived from assignment to assignment, the nervous equivalent of living from paycheck-to-paycheck. One expensive consequence has been his continuous search for new clients because, for several reasons and with few exceptions, he could not develop the rapport with clients that is necessary for repeat business. He met with me over lunch to ask me why.

"Well, you're a good writer, so your talent isn't the problem," I advised, and then told him about my bar, parties, golf games and so on. His reply: "I can't afford to do all that."

"Let's see," I said. "You can afford the horrendous costs of sitting around between jobs and not billing your time while searching for new customers. But you can't afford the relative pittance of hospitality, friendliness, call it what you want."

He argued: "It would take a long time for my investment in hospitality to pay off." "True," I said, "at least six months." "I can't wait that long," he replied, and I could see that he was stuck in the self-defeating paradigm of short-term thinking that guarantees mediocrity and frustration, and that is described in PART I. I gave up; he is still complaining years later that business is bad.

I asked two of my clients to comment on this chapter. "I recognize myself," they replied. One said that I should make a stronger case for my facilities. "I work with you to a great extent because we can really focus on the task at hand and let our creative juices flow when we meet there, away from the countless distractions of my offices." "I love our brainstorming sessions at your place," added the other, who meets here often with me and his designer, sometimes only with his designer.

Then, almost as an aside, one said that I was a pretty smooth writer too. Is the product less important than the ambiance surrounding it?

**

IN 2013: My life changed dramatically in ten years: one of my three primary corporate clients went bankrupt through mismanagement, and two others fell on hard times and cut their communications budgets, defying all logic. Three of the four managers I worked with most closely in those companies died; the fourth was downsized and remains one of my closest friends. My writing business with those firms disappeared.

But my principles haven't and won't. I still try to treat the people around me with all the generosity, dignity, and respect I can muster, and I still stick to my knitting of teaching and writing; creating rapport with everyone I know and meet. I still share the wealth with new and former clients and friends. In short, I still try to make 'em smile.

I've succeeded, mostly, and failed, more often than I'd like, a mixed bag. I've resigned from teaching at universities and developed several new and smaller clients, mostly for teaching but also for the occasional writing assignment. I helped a client write a huge proposal, missed the mark for reasons that I still do not understand and my client can't explain, and was fired. I published two books to what I refer to as wonderful reviews and woeful sales, and am writing three others as I write this. I coach an executive or two to improve their writing; one liked what I did for him, the other fired me for reasons that he refuses to divulge, which I find childish. I volunteer to sit on the publications committee of the Engineers Society of Western Pennsylvania and have been guest editor and contributor to its magazine, Pittsburgh Engineer, again to wonderful reviews. .

Most important, I've developed many new friends, most based on our professions. We all believe in and practice the power of dignity: I've purposely dropped those few that don't, won't, or can't.

The bottom line is simply this: I am as busy professionally and socially as ever. I think it's proof that treating people with dignity makes 'em smile, and that's good for everyone.

10. LESSONS LEARNED FROM LIFE ON A ROCKY ROAD

THIS SMALL MANUFACTURER OF VALVES HAS SURVIVED ON INNOVATION AND EMPLOYEE/CUSTOMER SATISFACTION. IT BARELY SURVIVED FIFTEEN YEARS AS A CASH COW.

Dick Conley is director of engineering at Kerotest Manufacturing Company, a designer and maker of valves used by distributors of natural gas, operators of power plants, and other similar industries. He is highly respected by his peers and customers for his engineering savvy, and has been employed by Kerotest for more than thirty years. He relates his experiences:

"I've learned a lot during my thirty-plus years here that supports the premise of this book, and which I've revisited and formalized while contributing to it. Customers indeed shape our and every other business, and the overarching purpose of every business is a satisfied customer. Employees are needed who recognize these basic truths and serve (some say delight) customers beyond their expectations, and those same employees are willing to work their tails off to do that if they know the goals and share in the success of the company. I've also learned that all physical assets stem from customers, a concept I had not understood consciously before, and I wonder how many people in business do. Profits and the value of the business inevitably jump when we work toward those ends. It all seems so simple, yet it all seems so elusive.

"I'm pleased to say that Kerotest adheres to many of the principles. For example, every employee, and I do mean every, shares in the company's fortunes. We became an ESOP in 1985—after more than fifteen years as a cash cow for a much larger company, a topic that I'll get into later—and everyone is given, at no cost, shares of stock as a yearly bonus. We don't have any outside owners. The value of a share is determined at the end of every calendar year by an independent auditor, and operating statements are posted every month for everyone to see. Our retirees all enjoy a nice nest egg through these gifts.

"Our workplace encourages employee satisfaction, and, as a result, customer satisfaction. We don't tolerate discrimination or harassment of any type; we encourage teamwork and our managers are open to suggestions for improving product quality, lowering costs and delivery times, and increasing safety, which is a very big deal here. Managers are also open to suggestions for new products that we could or should develop, and have a formal process for submitting and evaluating new product ideas. It's the idea that is evaluated, not the position of the submitter.

"Back to the workplace: We work in teams, and, as you'd expect, we encourage Total Quality Management and Continuous Improvement. No one works on trivial tasks such as creating slogans or banners or unnecessary reports, and we make sure that everyone knows that he or she is critical to getting the job done.

"We don't play favorites, with reserved parking, for example, and everyone dresses in business casual. And, of course, salaries and benefits are competitive. That's fundamental.

"On a more personal note, I love my work as a designer and inventor of valves. I'm an

engineer through and through, and management lets me be one without a lot of outside distractions.

"As for customer focus, point one in our contract with production workers is: Do what it takes to satisfy customers (no more 'it's not our job'). Point two is: Do it in a team environment (if you can't work as an effective team member, you can't work at Kerotest). Our administrative staff is acutely aware of these goals and works toward them as well.

"We've been modestly successful throughout much of our ninety-five year history; (survival alone is a measure of success, especially compared to many of our contemporary companies that no longer exist. Does anyone remember J&L Steel, the B&O, Hussey's and many, many others?). We'll celebrate our centennial in 2009, which I suppose says that we must be doing many things right.

"Four, years-long periods stand out as good examples of how employees and customers worked together closely for mutual satisfaction; I'll talk about them in chronological order.

"You could say that Kerotest, during the first half of the twentieth century, was key to developing America's oil fields and the oil industry, and by extension the age of the automobile. The low pressure of oil from the first shallow wells could be contained by the cast iron valves of the time. Then, as wells were drilled deeper into the earth, pressures increased and cast iron was just too weak for the job.

"Kerotest worked with the drillers to develop and test a cast steel valve that could. The valves were tested with kerosene under pressure, giving Kerotest its name. They quickly became the mainstay of the company's product line and the preferred valve in the oil fields, and held that position until World War II, when Kerotest was virtually taken over by the government and supplied countless valves for the war effort. In our absence, competitors took over the oilfield market, and Kerotest could not regain its share. But the company survived.

"That innovative kerosene test led to another in the sixties, when the nuclear business was in full swing. Many valves in nuclear plants were leaking borated, radioactive water through their stem packing, raising the radioactivity in the plants to dangerously unhealthy levels, requiring very expensive clean-up efforts. An engineer with Westinghouse—the leading builder of the plants at the time—discovered somehow that we had developed a packless valve, and called us in for a presentation. There was no question that our valves could stop the leaks, but could they handle the pressures, temperatures, and flows required? The higher pressure and temperature requirements were satisfied, but flow capacity was another matter.

"An independent lab made a mistake and overrated the flow capacity of the Kerotest valve. Our principle competitor discovered this mistake in our advertising and brought this to the attention of Westinghouse. In fact, they went so far as to perform a demonstration flow comparison test. They designed and set up a test that consisted of two tanks holding the same amount of water, one drained by the competitors' valve, another by our packless design. The test proved what they suspected and we learned: our valves could not handle as large a flow, but they didn't leak. So we and Westinghouse questioned if the flow specifications were realistic; were such large flows really needed? Wouldn't a slower rate be acceptable?

"Engineers from Westinghouse and the predecessor to the Nuclear Regulatory Commission reviewed the data and decided that flow rates could be reduced without jeopardizing the operations or safety of the plants, and we landed huge orders for our valves for many years—until the nuclear business collapsed in the early eighties.

"That success story was the direct result of employees and customers working together to solve a very serious problem. Everybody won: We did with higher sales, and Westinghouse and its customer, the NRC, with safer plants. And we've never heard a complaint about flow capacity or any other characteristic of our valves.

"Our involvement with the nuclear business surfaced again in 1980 when we bid on a government contract for 5000 valve sets to be installed in a huge uranium enrichment plant. Each set consisted of thirteen precision valves, seven self-actuated valves—the expensive kinds—and they had to snap shut or open in milliseconds. Together, the sets represented many millions in sales, and, if we were the successful bidder, the contract would be the biggest order in our history. Fifty other companies bid against us, and some were heavyweights like GE, Lockheed, and Borg Warner...all much bigger by far than Kerotest and all with physical and people assets that we could only imagine.

"Our management committed to the project, I was named head of the development team, our CEO convinced us that we could be the winner, and our bankers agreed to finance the new plant we'd need.

"With that sort of confidence and commitment, we worked around the clock for a year, established a close rapport with the customer, built prototypes that passed all the tests, and won the contract for half the sets. We invested several millions in a building and the necessary equipment, hired fifty people at attractive wages, and, within a year, began to ship production units. We filled the entire order on schedule over five years, greatly increasing our revenues and profits.

"We survived the ensuing fifteen years or so by serving our traditional markets, which eventually provided us with what we hope is our next big opportunity. During the past year we collaborated with our customers in the natural gas distribution business to design and manufacture a better, less expensive ball valve made of high-density polyethylene. The valves were designed using a new software program that allowed us to shave excess material without affecting pressure ratings. The result is a valve that is smaller, lighter, easier to install, and easier on customers' pocketbooks.

"The valves will be made at our plant in Louisiana, not overseas where many competitors have moved production, saving good jobs for Americans. And the early enthusiasm for the valves expressed by gas distributors is being expressed by water distributors and other industries. It's no wonder that our expectations for this product are high.

"The important point is that without the very close cooperation between our customers and designers, the valves would never have seen the light of day. We won with a new product line, our customers won with superior performance at a lower cost.

"Just this past month I was able to demonstrate again how customer involvement and satisfaction leads to sales. We are developing a new battery-powered electrofusion controller for use with polyethylene piping systems. After all sorts of internal debate about what customers want and are willing to pay for—two entirely separate questions and answers that enter into almost every purchasing decision—I met with a top engineer at our largest customer, a gas utility, and laid out the options. He was both surprised and delighted that we asked for his input (is it that unusual?) and influenced the design in ways that will surely broaden the marketability of the product. He promised to order more controllers from us, and volunteered to spread the word to his peers at other utilities. In essence, he has become an important arm of our marketing department, and we're gearing up for a surge in orders."

Courting Disaster with MBA-Think

Dick continued: "And now for the darker side. Back in the mid-sixties, Control Data Corporation (CDC), a maker of mainframe computers that was based in Minneapolis, bought Kerotest. The story of CDC's ownership demonstrates the opposing and negative mission of management, stockholder value.

"CDC bought Kerotest when it acquired Commercial Credit Corp. and they wanted to get into the business of making process control valves, an adjunct to their computer business. It was an OK idea (well ahead of its time), but it didn't work in practice simply because CDC's management was too focused on computers, which they figured would be the more profitable part of their business. So Kerotest, which in some years contributed one percent of sales and ten percent of profits to CDC, was basically ignored. By that I mean that requests for capital were brushed aside, so naturally our plants soon bordered on obsolete, and our R&D efforts withered. Kerotest became the proverbial 'cash cow'. We fed money to the dying mainframe business, and stagnated.

"Not knowing what else to do with this strange business, CDC sold Kerotest back to its employees just at the tail end of the boom in nuclear plant construction, when Kerotest's profits were at their peak. The timing was great for CDC—but not great enough, apparently, because CDC went out of business soon after—and terrible for Kerotest, which borrowed heavily to pay for the over-valued stock. The value of the stock has risen over the years, but not anywhere near as fast as the Dow; we are not a glamorous

140

business. Nevertheless, the stock is a wonderful perk for employees.

"The bottom line is simply this: When we are collaborating with customers to develop new products that solve problems or meet needs, we employees are satisfied and are happy to be working here. During these times, the company is quite profitable. When we lapse into that self-defeating paradigm of cost-cutting to be lean-and-mean, employees become fidgety and profits shrink. We have bounced back from several of those dismal times. The best course for management, our employees, and customers is, clearly, managing for satisfaction. Our history proves it."

Dick philosophized a bit after telling me this story of his company: "Your book is needed—you've hit on a great topic—and it's timely. It seems that we reward the scoundrels of the business world, and the good guys toil in obscurity. That's not right. Another point: Our young people think that performance in business is graded A, B, C, D, just as they were graded in school. In fact, there are only two grades in business, or there should be: 100 percent and fail, and I know that 100 percent, perfection, isn't possible all the time but it sure can be the goal. Think of it this way: If the janitor cleaning the floor leaves a pile of debris in the center, the floor is still dirty. If the heart surgeon cleans two of three arteries doing a triple bypass, the patient isn't cured or could die. If we make a marginal valve, it will always be marginal. We don't need that."

IN 2013, Dick is retired and all I know about Kerotest is that it is still in business. Nobody has returned my repeated calls to update its story, so, an opinion: Dick is the only person in the company who subscribes to the premise of this book. I wish the managers and the firm well.

11. I COULDN'T BELIEVE MY EARS!

A PREMIUM PRODUCT AT A PALATABLE PRICE YIELDS

PHENOMENAL GROWTH FOR THIS ENGINEERING FIRM.

Lovorn Engineering's founder, Ken Lovorn, explained how he formed and is growing his company: "I'll never forget it. I was in a meeting of about twenty top and middle managers of my former employer, an engineering and construction company that had been in business for about a century and employed some seven thousand people. The company's primary market, the steel industry in North America, was on its well-known skids, and orders for design and construction had shriveled both in number and size.

"The steel industry is dead," pontificated the president. "Nevertheless, we will continue to aggressively pursue new business from this, our traditional market. In fact, we will step up our sales and marketing."

"I couldn't believe my ears. Surely this man was not so mired in the past—stuck in his outdated paradigm—that he didn't realize his own contradiction. Surely he knew that the dead cannot be resurrected. Surely he knew that new markets needed to be pursued and opened if the company was to survive.

"I couldn't believe my ears for the second time as the managers applauded in homage to their so-called leader with an ostrich complex. Could the power to hire and fire be that much more potent than the power of simple reason? Did our president surround himself with 'yes' people? I answered my own questions: Yes, and of course he did.

"I flashed back to an article that I had read recently: one of the ten corporate sins that guarantee failure is 'fearing the boss more than the marketplace'. This company's managers practiced that sin to perfection. I also knew that all sorts of research concluded that smart employees privy to a reasonable amount of information—which we were and did—make better decisions than the smartest top executive. In this case, the 'smart' employees chose to sit on their tongues.

"The inevitable happened. A grand old name in engineering/construction went down the chute, and a grand new name, Lovorn Engineering, was born.

"I don't mean to imply that Lovorn Engineering was born because of my impulsive reaction to one event. Far from it, as my work history will confirm.

"I graduated, in 1970, from the University of Oklahoma with my degree in electrical engineering with special emphasis on logic circuit design. I immediately went with a design firm in Oklahoma City and was put in charge of the electricals of a three-million-square-foot office building. I figured I gained twenty years' experience in three years on that one project alone. Well, the company's workload dried up, so I moved to another design firm, this one headquartered in New York City with an office in DC, then to an architectural/engineering firm in Alexandria, Virginia. When the controller with that firm resigned I smelled something fishy, so I joined another firm, in Buffalo, and watched as my previous employer filed for bankruptcy.

"The owners of the firm in Buffalo didn't like my management style, whatever that very general comment means, and they never explained it so I guess they didn't know either. Truth be told, I didn't like their style either, especially when the top guy guaranteed me a bonus and then reneged without reason. It was then that I learned the importance of trust, of integrity in all relationships, including—especially—relationships with employees, and, of course, customers.

"So I landed with the firm with the ostrich as president. During my ten years there, I watched his management style, which boiled down to cutting costs despite jeopardizing the business's abilities to attract good employees and new customers with quality work. To be more specific, he would staff up when there was a big contract to work on, and lay off most of the worker bees—the designers, never the managers—when the workload was lower. And he set up a subsidiary in the Philippines to do the designs we did here in the States because costs per man hour were so low. What an illusion! Total costs actually rose when we in the states had to redo the shoddy designs produced by the overseas office, despite supervision by American designers sent there. I learned then that the folks putting lines on the paper or computer screen are key to the quality that customers expect and demand, and that cutting headcount can self-destruct the company.

"The result was an organization chart that looked more like a cylinder than a pyramid—there were almost as many managers as there were designers, and too many of the managers were cronies of the president and couldn't (wouldn't) be fired, giving respectability once again to the idea that hiring your friends can be destructive. And, as I've already noted, soon there were too few contracts to support the top-heavy structure.

"I somehow saw what was going on, and decided to get out from under managers bent on destruction of their companies, and destruction of their employees' lives, and do my own thing. After all, I reasoned, I had learned a great deal about what creates success and what creates failure, and I knew the difference.

"I wrote a business plan with the help of some new software—remember, I needed that software because I had spent most of my career as a designer and mid-level manager of design teams, not as a manager responsible for the revenue and profits of an entire firm.

"Writing the plan forced me to define my core mission for the business: to provide a premium product at a palatable price, thereby creating a competitive advantage based on value. I can remember when 'competitive advantage' and 'value' were the buzzwords of business. As is the way of buzzwords, they were replaced by others invented by consultants bent on doing the same thing under a new rubric. I'm from the old school; I feel that competitive advantage and value are timeless."

Core Values, Not Magical Results

"I realized then, just as I realize now, that my mission isn't new, that just about every business is on a similar tack whether it is expressed explicitly or not. I also realized that implementing the mission is the tough part, especially since engineering has become pretty close to being a commodity. We in the business know how difficult it is to sell 'better' or 'premium' just as it's difficult to sell peas or paper clips as 'better'. Difficult, but possible. So I arrived at what I call my core principles, convinced that they are the keys to continuity, growth, and profitability of my business.

"First, avoid greed, espouse contentment. Many years ago I discovered the guns/butter curve for governments. It says, quite simply, that all societies must find their balance of spending on guns [defense] and social betterment [butter] that the citizens are willing to accept. If spending for either guns or butter exceeds some undefined limit, then spending for one or the other must decline [or taxes or deficits must rise]. Officials at the top must then decide who to satisfy, the generals or the citizens.

"A similar search for an acceptable balance faces managers, except that the two curves are labeled 'customers' and 'employees'. The question then becomes 'how much should be invested to satisfy which group?' The simple answer for me is: 'more than my competitors'; satisfying both groups leads to competitive advantage and continuity of the business.

"Of course, something has to 'give' when investing more, and the 'give' for me is profits and managers' compensation, which, in the case of a small company like mine, can be one and the same. What never gives is compensation and benefits of employees who do the real work.

"Explaining this simple concept to my peers usually prompts retorts along the lines of sending me to their favorite shrink. After all, they reason, the point of every business is to maximize profits, a kissin' cousin to that awful mantra that has brought down so many businesses: stockholder value. My critics are both right and wrong: right in that I am as interested in profits as anyone, and wrong in that I will content myself with lower profits in exchange for continuity of the business—which means that my employees and customers can go about their lives without fear of my disrupting them with a decision based on greed.

"Second, strive for zero turnover of 'good' employees and customers, good employees being those who understand and agree to work within my core values, and good customers being those who recognize the value we bring to their businesses. The corollary to this is to strive for zero expense for recruiting and sales, two of the biggest eroders of profits for any business.

"We're close to meeting those goals. Our customers stick with us; repeat business is ninety percent of our total. But, in a perfect example of how employees and customers are intertwined, after almost three years in business, I had to let one of our twenty engineers go largely because of his insensitivity to a customer's needs, another because he for some unknown reason developed some pretty lax work habits.

"I hired the first engineer based on his fifteen years of solid experience, great references, and outstanding qualifications such as a professional engineers license. I never asked his previous employers how he got along with customers...I assumed he was OK there, and you know what the first three letters of 'assume' are.

"Anyway, I put this guy in charge of the electrical design for a small, three-story office building, and he overdesigned it big time. The electrical equipment rooms, one on each floor, were at least twice the size needed, raising the initial cost of the building, and, more importantly, reducing the space available for rental. That would cost the customer several thousand dollars a year for however long he owned the building. Unacceptable.

"I trusted this engineer so much that I didn't check the design before he sent it to the customer. That's a strike against me, isn't it?

"The customer called a meeting with the three of us, and pointed out the overdesign. I agreed. My engineer defended his design and refused to change it. I could hardly believe my ears, again. Neither could the customer: he was incensed, and had every right to be.

"So I redid the design myself within a crash schedule, costing my business thousands if you count the cost of the original and revised design. The actual cost was probably much higher: I and my customer advocate had to spend considerable time smoothing the ruffled feathers of the customer. If there's any good news in this story, it's that the customer, an architect/engineer with whom we've worked for years, has forgiven our foibles and is still working with us.

"This brings up a major point. I'm fond of saying that it costs nothing to keep a customer; all we have to do is the job we're contracted to do, and do it better than expected. We didn't do the job in this case, so the cost of keeping the customer was horrendous and unacceptable. Yet it was far lower—probably in the area of ten percent—than the cost to create a customer from scratch.

Are customers and employees my mother lode of assets? You bet. All my other assets—computers, desks, and so on—are derived from these two.

I implement the two principles above with several actions:

1. Pay designers at least five percent above the going rate, and recognize excellence with an even higher premium, and with awards such as company-paid dinners for the designer and his or her family.

2. Provide comfortable, people-friendly space for employees that encourages creativity and efficiency. For example, lighting levels are high enough to discourage fatigue, low enough to minimize the costs of power. And I installed a thermostat to control the temperatures in our space. Did you know that a study of comfort in offices concluded that employees generally are satisfied with temperatures if they can control them?

3. Offer ownership in the company to all employees by way of a very generous profit-sharing plan. In that way, all employees have a stake in how the company is managed, a vested interest that

assures their continuing involvement in the continuity of their careers and the careers of all other employees. It also fosters teamwork at all levels of the company, which leads inevitably to higher customer satisfaction and repeat business.

4. Believe—really believe—Peter Drucker when he said that customers determine what a business is, and behave accordingly by, first, giving each customer what I've come to call 'creative value.'—solutions that go beyond what customers ask for or think they need. An example: The specifications for an emergency electricity generating system at a hospital called for two generators. I presented statistical and engineering evidence to administrators that the hospital would be protected against catastrophic power outages much better if three generators were installed, and that the additional cost would be very nominal. They agreed, thanked me, and have rewarded our creativity with several contracts for other work.

Another example: we exceeded the expectations of a local bank on several projects so far that the bank's project managers actually revised our bid price upward on subsequent projects. They said we earned the premium. That's creative value at its best, and they are the kind of customer that recognizes and rewards it.

5. Retain one employee to be the 'customer advocate' in our office; ours owns twenty-five percent of the business, so he has a bigger financial stake than most employees in our drive to satisfy customers and grow the business. His first job is to know our customers so well that he can virtually read their minds so that our designs are shaped to match their needs as precisely as possible, or to exceed their needs when appropriate. I jokingly say that our customer advocate can be our customer zealot; he sometimes takes his job too seriously, if that's possible. For example, not long ago he got so carried away with satisfying one customer that he extended payment terms, severely hurting our cash flow. I suppose that's a good news, bad news story."

"Has implementing my principles worked well for us? Consider that we've grown—as measured by the number of employees and revenue—by 2000 percent during the past three years. Ninety percent of our business is repeat, and employee turnover during the company's formative years has been only five percent and is expected to be nil as we mature and continue to grow, albeit at a slower rate."

* * * *

P.S. I first called Ken Lovorn and asked him to contribute to this book after I read about him in the *People to Watch* column in the local paper. I found a man of extraordinary compassion; a man who adopted five young Russian orphans after traveling to Russia and somehow maneuvering through the maze of bureaucratic muck needed to give these children a better life. He told me that, statistically, two of his children are alive because he adopted them; about 40 percent of orphans in Russia die before their 21st birthday. By itself, it's a story of a life well spent. I think that his display of compassion has spilled over to his business, but he demurs: "I did nothing special," he'll tell you. I don't believe it. Do you?

**

IN 2013: Lovorn Engineering has expanded into larger offices and increased the number of employees by about 50 percent. The company is designing the electrical system for a multi-million dollar building at a nearby university, the largest contract the firm has ever booked. In addition, the firm has diversified into a related field by purchasing the franchise for a 3D printer, and quickly sold several units to local manufacturers and architects. All in all, Ken describes his business as "fabulous".

12. BEFORE AND AFTER. THE TAWDRY CLASH OF MANAGEMENT STYLES

FROM THE CALM OF NO LAYOFFS OR CUSTOMER DEFECTIONS FOR THIRTY-THREE YEARS TO THE CHAOS OF HEADCOUNT REDUCTION IN ONE EASY ACQUISITION.

X, an entrepreneur who prefers to remain anonymous, explains why: "The folks who bought my business will not hesitate to rattle my cage if I say anything negative about them." Suffice it to say that he is a successful businessman living in a small town in California. At age seventy-one, he is convinced that 'to retire is to expire,' and he'll 'probably be back in the saddle soon'. He is also convinced that many managers today 'just don't get it' with 'it' referring to the need for continuity based on satisfaction.

X is in a clash—a war if you prefer—of management ideologies that ignited when he sold his successful company to a huge conglomerate after its managers promised, at the bargaining table, to continue X's style of managing for the satisfaction of his triangle of employees, customers, and suppliers. The acquirers then decided, just after the final papers were signed, that they didn't really mean it. He spoke to me about his colorful experiences, particularly that deceit and its results:

"My style worked very well: absolutely no layoffs for the entire thirty-three years that I was in business. I know and like my employees and their families, visited the plants regularly to chat and find out how their lives were going. Layoffs of strangers are distasteful; layoffs of friends are repugnant. Management by walking around, I think the folks who wrote *In Search of Excellence* called it, and I was doing it long before the book came out.

If we lost a customer I can't remember who or when. We surely never lost one of the seventy customers that provided us with eighty percent of our business. Maybe we lost one or two of the other five thousand that provided us with the rest; I don't know. Regardless, we came very close to zero turnover of both employees and customers, and reveled and prospered in its lower costs. We were reasonably profitable, even when the general economy was down. If we weren't why would that conglomerate want to buy us?

"But—the buyers are so deluded, so arrogant, so sure that they have a lock on good management—that their first act when they took over was to change management styles to 'bottom line' or 'lean and mean' mania. Of course, that destroyed the culture I had spent most of my life building.

"The results, after only a few months of them at the helm, haven't been pretty. Sales have slumped as customers became aware that the close relationships they had with employees were no longer possible. They're buying from other companies with which they can at least have a chance of restoring those relationships. Heads— their terrible term that dehumanizes people by reducing them to heads without bodies or names—have been cut across the board, justified as cost-cutting that is necessary to 'save' the company, which everyone involved knows is bull; it's symptomatic of the short-term thinking that is so endemic with those who cannibalize a good business.

"The person who was president—a close friend of mine—couldn't live with the new climate of contention, and resigned in a huff. He was replaced by an accountant who knows nothing about the business or the people who operate it, everything about the numbers; there is a clear and important distinction between the two, and every manager with a scintilla of sense knows it. Other employees have told me that they are looking for a way to escape what they perceive to be a ship sinking with the overbearing weight of misguided decisions made by greedy managers. They no longer can see the secure and comfortable future that was once so clear and comforting.

"The number and ferocity of customer complaints are surging, and nobody's there to answer them. Even today, months after I sold the business, I'm getting calls from friends (customers) who are tearing their hair out in frustration. Quotes are now taking weeks to prepare instead of two-four hours. Shipments from stock now take one to three weeks when they once took only twenty-four hours. Why? Too-few service people, policy changes, computer 'updates' that extend the time needed to process orders (but supposedly lower the cost) but shorten the time needed to prepare a report for management. Can you believe it? Slower order processing and shipments, faster reporting of irrelevant financial data. Lord, who comes first?

"Now, faster than a speeding bullet, these misguided souls can get reports that show how many customers and how much business they've lost—all valuable information for those looking to justify even more self-destructive cost-cutting and headcount reduction. Idiocy.

"Managers are so busy cutting jobs and other costs that they can't respond, so they pass complaints off to lower-level employees. They call it 'delegating'—a BS term they learned at some MBA school with a fixation on numbers—which means that they don't want to hear the bad news themselves, a clear validation of how far removed they are from the actual day-to-day operations of the business. Then they're surprised when complaining customers complain even more.

"None of this type of decimation happens overnight, which head-counting and cost-cutting managers can't seem to understand. The raping of a company like mine—and I suppose any other—is like a cancer growing so slowly that it's not obvious to the managers who haven't a clue about the business's potential. Lost sales are dismissed for all the wrong reasons—the 'buyer quit', or 'the customer is loaded with inventory and isn't placing new orders', or 'the bad weather has killed production'. They never look at the real cause—their own vision and management style that are tilted in the wrong directions—so they never notice that the sky is falling.

"The vast difference between them and me is wrapped in one massive concept: relationships, and how they're built, maintained, and nurtured. To me, 'relationships' is the hook, the competitive advantage that allows entrepreneurs to succeed in this big tough world. As long as the ENRONs and TYCOs of the world don't understand that—and I for one don't think they ever will, with their heads stuck so solidly in the sands of numbers—there will always be room for people like me.

"Let me dig deeper. When I talk about relationships, I mean the close bonds to that triangle of employees, customers, and suppliers. By adding suppliers to the mix I'm intentionally broadening the focus of this book, unless you think of suppliers as employees, as I do. Like employees, good suppliers work for the success and continuity of the company. I haven't laid off a good supplier in years either.

"One reason that those in the triangle have endured is that I do not believe in secrets; everybody involved knows anything they want to know about the business, and, maybe, a lot that they don't care about. I never BS'd them: no secrets or lies, ever. Try that on a CEO of a giant company!

"Loyalty is another key. I've always stuck with those who brought me to the dance. I really believe that cliché, and live it with everybody in my triangle. I'm sure that if I take care of my triangle, sales and profits will take care of themselves, starting with sales. It's easier to push down from the top line of the operating statement than it is to push up from the bottom. My business has proven the truth in that: sales and profits have grown in lockstep at respectable rates, certainly faster than the industry we're in as a whole. All that has happened without a sales force; all of our business is repeat or from word-of-mouth from customer to customer, and often from supplier to customer. Isn't that another way of saying customer satisfaction?"

The Two Paths Open to Managers

"I see managers today as taking one of two ideological routes. The first is to focus on people skills, customer satisfaction, product integrity, and profits that are 'reasonable', which I think of as 'sufficient to sustain' the business. The second is cost-cutting, staff reduction, benefits-squeezing, and the like.

"I'm convinced that good managers will take the first path if they want to succeed over the longer term. It encourages creativity and strategic thinking, maximizes sales by raising customer acceptance levels, and elevates the capabilities of employees. None of that has anything to do with the second path, which is the one chosen by bad managers who intend to cannibalize the company. They prepare the company for acquisition by spinning the books to the best light, and the light stays lit for only a short time. In my value system, that's lying and cheating, and, over the long term, it inevitably leads to catastrophic drops in sales and profits, and soon the entire business goes down the drain and all sorts of lives are unnecessarily disrupted or destroyed.

"The list of corporate rapes seems to lengthen every day—and the managers responsible for them get the headlines that they don't want but they sure as hell deserve. Top managers line their own pockets and the troops are left with empty pockets and futures. Good managers avoid that kind of blatant chicanery."

**

IN 2013: I've lost track of X and I'm not surprised; he wanted to retire and live quietly on his estate in California. So we must take his story for the tawdry tale and lesson it is: that managing for profits, not people, destroys lives and businesses. Sustainability be damned!

PART III: CONNECTING THE DOTS; ENVISIONING THE FUTURE

Contributors to this book know that Dignity is a powerful management tool, perhaps the most powerful in their vast toolbox. They also know that, in a more perfect world, Dignity would be more universally applied.

13. THE COMMON THREADS

Contributors to this book share many values, strategies, and tactics that contribute to success

A student of mine once wrote an essay on the purpose of management. She concluded that *continuity* was the key concept, and went on to support it with the economic and societal benefits of continuity of the organization, which of course led to continuity of the countless lives that rely on the organization for their well-being. If we think continuity, she reasoned, the cold numbers of profit, ROI, and stock price would fall into place.

She got it right, just as the contributors to this book have it right.

Management is, first and foremost, about people, and managing for stockholder value enables managers to forget that simple axiom, or to put it on the back burner. When managers talk about common culture, shared vision, continuous learning, customer satisfaction—you know the basketful of buzzwords—they are talking about people, and I see a three-way tie for the three groups vying for the title of most important. Employees, of course, because all these concepts pertain to them, including customer satisfaction; customers because they are the reason for the organization; and then there are the people in the background, surely the largest group: families, friends, suppliers, and businesspeople supplying ancillary services.

Contributors to this book have tilted their management style strongly toward Dignity as the route to Sustainable Competitive Advantage in the following ways. Perhaps, if you agree with the tilt, your challenge is to incorporate their insights into your style and mission.

1. Employees are hired for their fit into the culture as much or more than for their technical skills. As a result:

• Turnover is so low that managers don't bother to measure it; their best guess is that it less than two percent a year, vs. about 25 percent for all businesses in the United States. Recruiting expense is low.

- Productivity is so high that the business can afford to pay above the average rate for comparable jobs.

- Continuous learning is the norm, helping to assure technical competence.

2. Customers are respected by all employees, even those without direct responsibilities for working with them. As a result:

- Repeat business is extraordinarily high, above 95 percent, as customers' expectations are exceeded.

- Sales expense is low, close to zero or commensurate with growth of revenues.

3. Guiding principles include:

- Active listening to employees and customers to understand their needs and wants.

- Truth in all communications and dealings.

- Fun on the job whenever and wherever possible.

14. EPILOGUE AND PROLOGUE: TOWARD UNIVERSAL ACCEPTANCE

SPREADING THE WORD ABOUT DIGNITY CAN IMPROVE THE PUBLIC'S AND GOVERNMENT'S PERCEPTION OF BUSINESS

Here is a modest call to action that, admittedly, is my attempt to start stakeholders talking constructively about infusing Dignity into business worldwide. I want to start with two simple steps; stakeholders can:

1. Put the blame on business failures where it belongs most often: On the top managers who are approved by boards who are elected by shareholders. Therefore, executives, board members, and

shareholders are ultimately responsible for failures, and they should be held responsible for cleaning up the carnage they cause.

2. Insist that prudent managers prepare for the unlikely but possible future by creating trust/transition funds, preferably with the active participation of enlightened governments. The funds can be used to train displaced employees, and to help support affected communities.

The pervasive ideal among contributors to this book is that treating stakeholders with dignity is the driver of financial and social success. The contributors aren't alone. Costco's' chairman has said that, "We think that when you take care of your customer and your employees, your shareholders are going to be rewarded in the long run. I care about the stock price. But we're not going to do something for the sake of one quarter that's going to destroy the fabric of our company and what we stand for."

Caterpillar's chairman wrote in a recent annual report: "This is a company that knows financial results aren't all that matters. Developing, rewarding, and motivating people to ever-higher levels of achievement is just as important ... and integral to our continuing success...."I agree, and now that you've read this book, I hope that you do too. Pete Geissler

APPENDIX I: SUGGESTED FURTHER READING

AMERICAN SPIRIT: Visions of a New Corporate Culture, by Lawrence Miller

CAUSE FOR SUCCESS: Ten Companies that Put Profit Second and Come in First, by Christine Arena

GOOD COMPANY: Business Success in the Worthiness Era, by Laurie Bassi, Ed Frauenheim, and Dan McMurrer, with Larry Costello

IDEAS HAVE CONSEQUENCES, by Leonard Weaver

IN SEARCH OF EXCELLENCE: Lessons from America's Best-Run Companies, by Thomas J. Peters and Robert H. Waterman Jr.

PEAK: How Great Companies Get Their Mojo from Maslow, by Chip Conley

SUCCESS BUILT TO LAST: Creating a Life that Matters, by Jerry Porras, Stewart Emery, and Mark Thompson

THE NEW REALITIES: In Government and Politics/In Economics and Business/In Society and World View, by Peter Drucker

THE RESPECT EFFECT: Using the Science of Nreuroleadership to Inspire a More Loyal and Productive Workplace, by Paul Meshanko

ABOUT THE AUTHOR

Pete Geissler is a freelance professional writer who specializes in management/leadership, engineering/science, and energy/environmental issues. He is deeply concerned about the poor and deteriorating image of business held by the general public and governments, which he feels can be reversed by broadening g the mindsets of managers to be more thoughtful and humane-- without compromising profitability.

In *The Power of Dignity*, Mr. Geissler decries managing for stockholder value as a destructive philosophy, and proposes replacing it with Managing for Dignity. He offers solid empirical and anecdotal evidence that doing so creates sustainable competitive advantage.

The first edition of *Dignity*, published in 2004 as *Managing with Conscience for Competitive Advantage,* was a Finalist, Best Books 2004, awarded by USA Book News, with this comment: "This wonderful title suggests a management direction that could prevent more of the same large-scale failings (such as the Enron debacle) and restore a sense of social consciousness to management."

John Burroughs, Reviewer, Midwest Book Review, added: "More than just an ethical handbook, (this book) is a 'must read' chock full of prosperity-building tips, tricks, and techniques for small and big business managers alike."

Don Nusser, Vice President, Hatch Mott MacDonald, agrees: "Powerfully convincing ... a vastly important, necessary change to the way businesses could and should be led ... mandatory reading for executives worldwide."

***

The Power of Dignity is the first of Pete Geissler's leadership books; all are connected thematically by their single purpose: *to be the thinking leader's model for sustainable competitive advantage.* The second book is *The Power of Writing Well,* followed by *The Power of Ethics.*

Leaders who understand and practice these three foundational bulwarks will enhance the productivity, profitability, and competitive advantage of their organizations.

The books were born from insights derived from more than forty years consulting with leaders of various businesses and professional associations.

Mr. Geissler's other books include: *The Power of Being Articulate; The Power of Writing Well; Divorce can be Such Sweet Sorrow,* and *BigShots' Bullshit, The All-New Edition.*

For more: www.peteswords.com, and www.thexpressivepress.com